Grammar Made Easy

知っておきたい基礎英文法

Mikiko Hirata
Yoko Harada
Eric Bray

音声ファイルのダウンロード/ストリーミング

CD マーク表示がある箇所は、音声を弊社 HP より無料でダウンロード/ストリーミングすることができます。トップページのバナーをクリックし、書籍検索してください。書籍詳細ページに音声ダウンロードアイコンがございますのでそちらから自習用音声としてご活用ください。

https://www.seibido.co.jp

Grammar Made Easy

Copyright © 2014 by Mikiko Hirata, Yoko Harada, Eric Bray

All rights reserved for Japan.
No Part of this book may be reproduced in any form
without permission from Seibido Co., Ltd.

はしがき

　英語の文章を読まなければならないとき、とりあえず知っている単語を見つけてそれらを適当につなげ、何とか意味が通じる文に訳してみよう…というアプローチを繰り返し使ってきた人もいるかもしれません。どうしてもわからないとき、何とかして意味をとろうと努力をすること自体は悪いことではないのですが、そのような文法を無視した読み方では「当たる」ときもあるけれど「外れる」ことも多く、あまり自信を持って読むことができません。

　文法は、語と語がどのように結び付くのか、語がどんなふうに形を変えるのかなどに関するルールです。このルールを理解してその知識を生かすと、文の中で語句がどうつながって「かたまり」を作り、それぞれの「かたまり」がどう関係し合っているかが見えてきます。そして、複雑に見える文でも基本的な構造は実は単純で、決して手が付けられないほど難しいものではないことが分かってくるでしょう。

　この教科書では、各ユニットの1ページ目が文法の解説になっています。このページはただ読むだけでなく、一部はエクササイズのようになっており、自分で答えを書き込んで説明を完成させるようになっています。受け身にではなく、自ら積極的にルールを理解しようと取り組んでもらえるようにこのような形式にしました。文法の練習問題の他に、各ユニットの文法項目に即した100語程度のリーディング問題や暗唱文集も付いています。別売りのCDを利用しながら、複数の角度からトレーニングを繰り返し、定着を図ってください。

　本書での学習を通じ、今まで知識があいまいであった部分がはっきりとした形でまとまり、「もっと英語が勉強したい」と思っていただければ幸いです。

　最後になりますが、今回の教科書作成にあたり、貴重なアドバイスとサポートをくださった㈱成美堂の菅野英一氏に心よりお礼を申し上げます。

2014年6月　　　　　　　　　　　　　　　　　　　　　　　　　　著者一同

CONTENTS

Unit 1	品詞	1
Unit 2	5文型	5
Unit 3	代名詞	9
Unit 4	時制（1） 過去・現在・未来	13
Unit 5	助動詞	17
Unit 6	時制（2） 進行形	21
Unit 7	受動態	25
Unit 8	時制（3） 現在完了形	29
Unit 9	否定文	33
Unit 10	疑問文	37
Unit 11	比較級・最上級	41
Unit 12	副詞の働きをする（1） 前置詞＋名詞	45
Unit 13	副詞の働きをする（2） to 不定詞	49
Unit 14	副詞の働きをする（3） 接続詞＋節	53
Unit 15	形容詞の働きをする（1） 前置詞＋名詞	57
Unit 16	形容詞の働きをする（2） 分詞	61
Unit 17	形容詞の働きをする（3） to 不定詞	65
Unit 18	形容詞の働きをする（4） 関係代名詞節－1	69
Unit 19	形容詞の働きをする（5） 関係代名詞節－2	73
Unit 20	名詞の働きをする（1） to 不定詞	77
Unit 21	名詞の働きをする（2） 動名詞	81
Unit 22	名詞の働きをする（3） that 節と疑問詞節	85
	暗唱文（recitation）	89

Unit 1 品詞

基本的な品詞には、形容詞、副詞、接続詞、名詞、前置詞、代名詞、動詞があります。

◇リストから（　　）に当てはまる品詞を選び、下線部には各品詞の単語をあと3つずつ書きましょう。

　　　形容詞　　副詞　　接続詞　　名詞　　前置詞　　代名詞　　動詞

1. （　　　　）人や物事の名前を表す　　　　　　　　　student, door
　　　　　　　　　　　　　　　　　　　　　　　　　　_____

2. （　　　　）名詞の代わりをする　　　　　　　　　　I, his
　　　　　　　　　　　　　　　　　　　　　　　　　　_____

3. （　　　　）動作を表す　　　　　　　　　　　　　　eat, like
　　　　　　　　　　　　　　　　　　　　　　　　　　_____

4. （　　　　）名詞を修飾したり、状態を表す　　　　　big, happy
　　　　　　　　　　　　　　　　　　　　　　　　　　_____

5. （　　　　）動詞、形容詞、副詞、文などを修飾　　　beautifully, always
　　　　　　　　する
　　　　　　　　　　　　　　　　　　　　　　　　　　_____

6. （　　　　）名詞の前に置いて、時や場所などを　　　during, under
　　　　　　　　表す
　　　　　　　　　　　　　　　　　　　　　　　　　　_____

7. （　　　　）語と語、文と文などを結ぶ　　　　　　　and, if
　　　　　　　　　　　　　　　　　　　　　　　　　　_____

A _____ に入る単語をリストの中からすべて選び、それらの単語の品詞を書きましょう。文頭の文字が小文字表記になっている場合があります。

we   slowly   good   with   and   drink   yesterday
Beth   buy   or   for   make   students   fast   new

1. I _____ coffee every morning.
   _____ → 品詞_____

2. We went to a _____ restaurant.
   _____ → 品詞_____

3. John made a chair _____ his brother.
   _____ → 品詞_____

4. My father ran _____ .
   _____ → 品詞_____

5. Tom _____ Cathy will come tomorrow.
   _____ → 品詞_____

6. _____ should study hard.
   _____ → 品詞_____
   _____

B 下線の単語の品詞を書きましょう。

1. We walk in the park every morning.　(　　　　)
2. We take a walk in the park every morning.
　　　　　　　　　　　　　　　　　(　　　　)
3. I worked hard.　　　　　　　　　(　　　　)
4. This is a hard question.　　　　　(　　　　)
5. Philanthropists help poor people.　(　　　　)
6. The students and the teacher stretched their arms.
　　　　　　　　　　　　　　　　　(　　　　)
7. The classroom is quite big.　　　　(　　　　)

C 各文中の形容詞は○で、副詞は□で囲みましょう。

1. This is an easy question.
2. I found the library easily.
3. Harry went to bed early.
4. Jim and I had an early dinner.
5. The dress was pretty.
6. The dress was pretty expensive.
7. I bought a very expensive hat.
8. Maria is a friendly person.
9. The new students really enjoyed the party tonight.
10. The store is still open.

D レストランのランチメニューを見て、問題に答えましょう。 02

```
A. Shrimp in spicy sauce      ￥1,000
B. Italian meatballs          ￥1,100
C. Chicken on skewers         ￥850
D. Stir-fried vegetables      ￥980

All dishes come with soup or salad, and rice.
```

1. メニューから次の品詞の語を [   ] 内の数だけ見つけましょう。

   a. 名詞　　[10] _____

   _____

   b. 形容詞　[4] _____

   c. 動詞　　[1] _____

   d. 前置詞　[3] _____

   e. 接続詞　[2] _____

2. 次の質問に答えましょう。

   a. シーフードを食べたい人はどれを注文するでしょう。　　(　　　)

   b. シーフードと肉が食べられない人はどれを注文するでしょう。(　　　)

Unit 2 5文型

英文の主な構成要素、主語（S）、述語動詞（V）、目的語（O）、補語（C）には決まった並べ方があります。

◇リストから各文型の文を選んで［　　］に書きましょう。

> Jimmy bought a jacket.　　He looks happy.　　Mary made me breakfast.
> My sister named the dog Sora.　　We cried.

第1文型　SV（SとVで成り立つ文）　　The girl runs.
　　　　　　　　　　　　　　　　　　［　　　　　　　　　　　］

第2文型　SVC（「S＝C」の文）　　　John was a teacher.
　　　　　　　　　　　　　　　　　　［　　　　　　　　　　　］

第3文型　SVO（「SがOをVする」　　I borrow a book.
　　　　　の文）　　　　　　　　　　［　　　　　　　　　　　］

第4文型　SVO₁O₂　　　　　　　　　My grandfather bought me the bag.
　　　　（「SがO₁にO₂をVする」　　［　　　　　　　　　　　］
　　　　の文）

第5文型　SVOC　　　　　　　　　　The news made me sad.
　　　　（「O＝C」の文）　　　　　　　［　　　　　　　　　　　］

＊5文型の文に修飾する言葉を付け加えると文の内容を豊かにすることができます。
　<u>I</u> sometimes <u>buy</u> foreign <u>magazines</u> there.
　S　　　　　　V　　　　　　O

5

A 前ページの例文の下線部分からS、V、O、Cを抜き出しましょう。
また、S、V、O、Cとなっている語の品詞を書きましょう。

S （例）(The) girl, _____ ( ) ( )

_____

V _____ ( )

O _____ ( ) ( )

C _____ ( ) ( )

B 語句を並べかえて英文を完成させましょう。文頭の文字が小文字表記になっている場合があります。

1. [baby / crying / is / the].

   _____ _____ on the sofa.
         S   V

2. [a / became / my / pilot / sister].

   _____ _____ _____ last year.
       S   V   C

3. [game / will / Ted / the / win].

   _____ _____ _____ tomorrow.
       S   V   O

4. [a / gave / he / me / ring].

   _____ _____ _____ _____ for my birthday.
     S   V   O   O

5. [open / leaves / door / the / he].

   _____ always _____ _____ _____ .
      S   V   O   C

C　リストから適切な語句を選び文を完成させましょう。同じ語句を繰り返し使う事はできません。

> can ski　　beer　　sleepy　　her　　wrote　　became　　named
> Rocky and Bunny　　drinks　　an e-mail　　the rabbits

1. He _____.
　　　　　V

2. He _____ _____.
　　　　　V　　　　　　　　C

3. He _____ _____.
　　　　　V　　　　　　　　O

4. He _____ _____ _____ yesterday.
　　　　　V　　　　　　　　O　　　　　　　　O

5. He _____ _____ _____.
　　　　　V　　　　　　　　O　　　　　　　　C

D　下線部の文型を書きましょう。

1. <u>My brother and I walk</u> to school.　　(　　　　　)
2. <u>I walk my dog</u> every morning.　　(　　　　　)
3. <u>We will keep the secret</u>.　　(　　　　　)
4. <u>We will keep the room clean</u>.　　(　　　　　)

E クイズを読んで、問題に答えましょう。　CD 03

　One day, ᵃa father gave his son a fox, a chicken and some corn. He said, "Take the fox, the chicken and the corn to the other side of the river. You can use the boat at the river. The boat is very small. ᵇYou can take yourself and only one of the three things at a time. But be careful. You can't leave the fox alone with the chicken because the fox will eat the chicken. You can't leave the chicken alone with the corn because the chicken will eat the corn." How can his son get everything across the river safely?

注) **the other side** 反対側　　　**at a time** 一度に

1. 各文の太字部分の、主語（S）、述語動詞（V）、目的語（O）、補語（C）に下線を引いて、S、V、O、C を書きましょう。

    ⓐ　One day, **a father gave his son a fox, a chicken and some corn**.

    ⓑ　**You can take yourself and only one of the three things** at a time.

2. 下の順番で運べば狐、鶏、トウモロコシをうまく向こう岸まで運ぶことができます。リストから適切な語句を選び、（　　　）に入れましょう。答えは 2 通りあります。繰り返し使う語句もあります。

    ┌───┐
    │　alone　　chicken　　with the chicken　　corn　　fox　│
    └───┘

    1. He takes the (　　　　　　) to the other side of the river.
    2. He comes back (　　　　　　).
    3. He takes the (　　　　　　) over.
    4. He comes back (　　　　　　).
    5. He takes the (　　　　　　) over.
    6. He comes back (　　　　　　).
    7. He takes the (　　　　　　) over.

Unit 3 代名詞

> 代名詞は、人称、格、単数複数によって形が決まります。

◇表の（　　）に適切な語を入れましょう。

	人称	主格	所有格	目的格
単数	1　私	I	my	（　　）
	2　あなた	you	（　　）	you
	3　「私・あなた」以外	he	（　　）	him
		she	her	（　　）
		it	（　　）	it
複数	1　私たち	we	our	（　　）
	2　あなたたち	（　　）	your	you
	3　「私たち・あなたたち」以外	they	（　　）	them
		主語(S)になる	後ろに名詞がくる	目的語(O)になる

◇　　　　　に入るのは主格・所有格・目的格のどれでしょう。

This is 　　　　 toy.　　　　　　　　　　　　　＿＿＿格

　　　　 am a student / is a student / are students.　＿＿＿格

The dog likes 　　　　　　　　　　　　　　　　＿＿＿格

＊目的格は前置詞の後ろにも来ます。
　I bought the jacket **for him**.

A 代名詞の所有格とそれに続く名詞を○で囲みましょう。

1. Your cat is cute.
2. The boys came to our house.
3. We met their teacher there.
4. I gave her my book.
5. Tom and his sister call the bird Tweetie.

B 日本語に合うように（　　）に適切な代名詞を入れて、全文を書きましょう。

（　　）invited（　　）to the party.

(例) 私　　あなた　　I invited you to the party．

1. 彼女　　私達　　＿＿＿＿＿＿＿＿＿＿＿＿＿＿＿＿＿＿．
2. 私達　　彼ら　　＿＿＿＿＿＿＿＿＿＿＿＿＿＿＿＿＿＿．
3. 彼ら　　あなた達　＿＿＿＿＿＿＿＿＿＿＿＿＿＿＿＿＿＿．
4. 彼　　　彼女　　＿＿＿＿＿＿＿＿＿＿＿＿＿＿＿＿＿＿．

C （　　）内から適切な語を選び、○で囲みましょう。

1. I need (he, his, him) e-mail address.
2. (They, Their, Them) are in New York now.
3. The music made (we, our, us) happy.

4. (We, Our, Us) school is near the station.

5. He did my homework for (I, my, me).

D (　　) 内から適切な語を選び、○で囲みましょう。

1. The children like (my, her, they) very much.

2. We talked about (she, it, our).

3. We asked (my, our, them) some questions.

4. I cooked and (she, me, him) washed the dishes.

5. Her car is old, but (its, their, it) tires are new.

E 下線部を適切な代名詞にかえて、全文を書きましょう。

1. The apartment looks nice.　　　_____

2. This is Janet's father.　　　_____

3. I take a walk with my brother.　　　_____

4. I showed the pictures to Ken.　　　_____

5. June and I are friends.　　　_____

F (　　) に適切な代名詞を入れましょう。

1. I read the book. (　　) was very interesting.

2. Anna and Emma are twins. (　　) birthday is September 8.

3. Mr. Brown is our neighbor. We know (　　) very well.

G ストーリーを読んで、問題に答えましょう。 04

I'm a nurse. I work in a hospital in America. American hospitals have some rules. One rule is: Doctors cannot operate on (a)**their** children.

One day, a nurse came in and said to us, "A father and (b)**his** son were in a car accident. (c)**They** are in our hospital now. The father has a broken leg and is in bed now. The son has a serious injury and needs an operation."

So we got ready for (d)**it**. Soon, a doctor came in, looked at (e)**him** and said, "(f)**I** can't operate on him. He is my son."

注) **operate on** 〜を手術する　　　**serious injury** 重症

1. 太字の代名詞は何を指しているか、日本語で答えましょう。

   ⓐ their _____
   ⓑ his _____
   ⓒ They _____
   ⓓ it _____
   ⓔ him _____
   ⓕ I _____

2. 下線部と同じ意味になるように I am で始まる文に書き直しましょう。
   "I am (　　　　　) (　　　　　)."

Unit 4 時制（1）過去・現在・未来

> 過去形と現在形は一般動詞や be 動詞の形をかえて作ります。未来形は will ＋動詞の原形で表します。

一般動詞

◇（　　　）内の動詞を適切な形にかえて文を完成させましょう。

時制	作り方	例文	
過去	原形の最後に -ed をつける	I ＿＿＿＿ the dishes.	(wash)
	不規則な変化をする	I ＿＿＿＿ an e-mail.	(write)
現在	動詞の原形をそのまま使う	I ＿＿＿＿ a song.	(sing)
	動詞の原形に -s をつける（主語が3人称単数の場合）		
		She ＿＿＿＿ a song.	(sing)
未来	will ＋動詞の原形で表す	We ＿＿＿＿ our best.	(do)
		Chris ＿＿＿＿ his best.	(do)

be 動詞

◇（　　　）に適切な be 動詞を入れましょう。

時制	条件	例文
過去	主語が I と 3 人称単数の時	Jun (　　　) a student.
	主語がそれ以外の時	We (　　　) students.
現在	主語が I の時	I (　　　) a student.
	主語が 3 人称単数の時	She (　　　) a student.
	主語がそれ以外の時	You (　　　) a student.
未来	主語が何であっても	They (　　　) students.

＊未来を表わすのに will の他に is/am/are going to があります。
　It will rain tomorrow. = It is going to rain tomorrow.

A ( ) 内の動詞を過去形、現在形、未来形にして書き直しましょう。

1. He (play) baseball.

   過去形 _____ last Sunday.

   現在形 _____ every Tuesday.

   未来形 _____ this weekend.

2. We (eat) rice and miso soup.

   過去形 _____ this morning.

   現在形 _____ every morning.

   未来形 _____ tomorrow morning.

3. Pat and Ben (be) tired.

   過去形 _____ last night.

   現在形 _____ all the time.

   未来形 _____ this evening.

B ( ) 内の動詞を過去形にして文を完成させましょう。

1. I _____ up at six yesterday morning.　　(get)
2. The teacher _____ the door open.　　(leave)
3. We _____ a psychology course last year.　　(take)
4. Maki and Zoe _____ together.　　(come)
5. She _____ me some cookies.　　(give)
6. They _____ the news on the radio.　　(hear)

C （　）内の動詞を正しい形にして文を完成させましょう。

1. I _____ my teacher yesterday.　　　　(call)
2. She _____ a computer last Friday.　　(buy)
3. My friends _____ in the library now.　(be)
4. Our father _____ 48 next year.　　　　(be)
5. Adam _____ home at four every day.　(come)
6. Jeff and I _____ the work tomorrow.　(finish)

D 各文を is/am/are going to を使って、全文を書き直しましょう。

1. The meeting will finish before 11.
   _____

2. Sandy's parents will enjoy the trip.
   _____

3. It will snow tomorrow.
   _____

4. I will be back soon.
   _____

E ある学生についての文章を読んで、問題に答えましょう。

　　Kenta loves traveling. He works part-time and earns 500,000 yen a year. He ⓐ(go) to a foreign country every spring and summer. He always ⓑ(spend) 50% of his annual earnings on his trips. This spring he went to Korea. He ⓒ(pay) 20,000 yen for flights and other transportation. The hotel fee ⓓ(be) 15,000 yen. He spent 7,000 yen on food. He also ⓔ(buy) some gifts for his family and friends. The trip cost 45,000 yen in all. This summer he is going to visit a friend in America. Kenta ⓕ(stay) with him, so he will not spend much money on this trip.
注）**annual earnings**　年収　　　　　**transportation**　交通手段

1. (　　) 内の動詞を適切な時制に直しましょう。
   ⓐ go ＿＿＿＿＿＿＿＿　　ⓑ spend ＿＿＿＿＿＿＿＿
   ⓒ pay ＿＿＿＿＿＿＿＿　　ⓓ be ＿＿＿＿＿＿＿＿
   ⓔ buy ＿＿＿＿＿＿＿＿　　ⓕ stay ＿＿＿＿＿＿＿＿

2. 次の質問に答えましょう。
   a. 健太は春の旅行でおみやげにいくら使いましたか。
   ＿＿＿＿＿＿＿＿＿＿＿＿＿＿＿＿＿＿＿＿＿＿＿＿＿＿＿＿＿＿＿＿＿＿

   b. 韓国旅行の後、今年のアメリカ旅行用の予算はいくら残っていますか。
   ＿＿＿＿＿＿＿＿＿＿＿＿＿＿＿＿＿＿＿＿＿＿＿＿＿＿＿＿＿＿＿＿＿＿

Unit 5 助動詞

> 助動詞とは、動詞にそれだけでは表せない色々なニュアンスを付け加えるもので、will、should、may、can、must などがあります。助動詞の後ろには動詞の原形がきます。

◇（　　　）に適切な語句を入れましょう。

助動詞	意味	例文	日本語訳
will	～だろう	The students will pass the test.	学生達は試験に合格するだろう。
can	～できる ～してもよい	I (　　　　　). You (　　　　　) home.	私は泳げる。 あなたは家に帰ってもよい。
may	～してもよい ～かもしれない	You (　　　　　) my car. They (　　　　　) here.	あなたは私の車を使ってもよい。 彼らはここに来るかもしれない。
must	～しなければならない ～に違いない	We (　　　　　) hard. He (　　　　　) angry.	私達は一生懸命勉強しなければならない。 彼は怒っているに違いない。
should	～すべきである	We (　　　　　) up early.	私達は早く起きるべきだ。

＊「～できる」の can は is/am/are able to 、「～しなければならない」の must は have/has to で表すこともできます。

◇（　　　）に適切な語句を入れましょう。
Brian can dance well.　　＝　Brian (　　　　　) dance well.
You must do your homework.　＝　You (　　　　　) do your homework.

A 日本語の文に合うように（　　）に適切な語を入れましょう。

1. マシューはとても眠いに違いない。

   Matthew (　　　) be very sleepy.

2. 明日サリーと遊園地に行ってもいいよ。

   You (　　　) go to the amusement park with Sally tomorrow.

3. 私達は5時までに仕事を終えなければならない。

   We (　　　) to finish this work by 5.

4. 私の犬は私の言っていることを理解できます。

   My dog (　　　) understand my words.

5. その宿題は彼らには難しすぎるかもしれない。

   The homework (　　　) be too difficult for them.

B 英文を日本語に訳しましょう。

1. The train leaves at 3:00, so you must arrive at the station before 2:50.

2. You should be quiet in the movie theater.

3. You may watch TV, but you have to finish your homework first.

4. I was able to read only 50 words per minute last year.

C 日本語の文に合うように語句を並びかえて英文を完成させ、全文を書きましょう。文頭の文字が小文字表記になっている場合があります。

1. 私達はここに車をとめるべきだ。
   [car / park / we / here / should / our].

2. 私のドレスをパーティに着て行ってもいいよ。
   [can / my dress / the party / to / you / wear].

3. ランディは彼の家族の世話をしなければならない。
   [care / family / has / his / of / Randy / take / to].

D （　　）内の助動詞を加えて全文を書き直しましょう。

1. Kaoru gets up early every morning.　　　　(must)

2. My dog is hungry.　　　　(may)

3. The students are able to sing English songs.　　　　(will)

4. He carries the box carefully.　　　　(should)

E 2人の学生のスケジュールについての文章を読んで、問題に答えましょう。

06

Mike has to write a paper in Japanese, and he is going to get help from his friend Ayaka. It will take 30 minutes.

Ayaka's first class is from 9:00 to 10:30. She is free during the second and third periods, but she has a badminton club meeting from 12:30. It usually takes 30 minutes. She is captain of the team, so (a)she must attend it. She has just one class in the afternoon from 3:00.

Mike's first class begins at 1:20, but he has to meet Professor Yano at 10:30. (b)It will take about an hour.

Both Ayaka and Mike finish their last classes at 4:30. Mike is free after that, but Ayaka has to work. She applied for a job at the on-campus bookstore, and fortunately she was able to get it. Her job starts at 6:00 and she should be at the bookstore by 5:50.

注) **paper** レポート　　　**apply for** ～に応募する　　　**on-campus** 学内の

1. 下線部内の助動詞を他の表現にかえて全文を書きかえましょう。

    ⓐ _____

    ⓑ _____

2. 綾佳がマイクを手伝うとしたら、いつですか。下の表に2人のスケジュールを書き込んで可能性のある時間帯を2つ挙げましょう。

	9	10	11	12	1	2	3	4	5	6
Mike										
Ayaka										

_____ と _____

20

Unit 6 時制（2）進行形

> 進行形は動作が進行していることを表し、be 動詞＋動詞の -ing 形（現在分詞）で作ります。時制は be 動詞で表します。

◇（　　　）に適切な語句を入れて、日本語に訳しましょう。

	例文	日本語訳
現在進行形	Dave（　　　　）studying English now.	デーブは今英語を勉強しています。
過去進行形	We（　　　　）watching TV at that time.	（　　　　　　　　　　　　）
未来進行形	I（　　　　）sleeping at 11:00 tonight.	（　　　　　　　　　　　　）

◇下の動詞を現在分詞に直して、表に書きましょう。

> run　play　sit　keep　come　give　stay
> stop　visit　study　use　begin　write

基本	子音字＋e で終わる	アクセントのある短母音＋子音字で終わる
そのまま -ing	-e をとって -ing	最後の子音を重ねて -ing
例）going	making	cutting

＊ know、like のような状態を表す動詞は、通常進行形では使われません。
　例）○　I know him.　　　×　I am knowing him.

A リストから適切な動詞を選び、-ing 形にかえて（　　　）に入れましょう。同じ語を繰り返し使う事はできません。

> snow　　drive　　swim　　shop　　study

1. Mr. Rogers was (　　　　　　　) a truck at that time.
2. The girls are (　　　　　　　) at the store.
3. I will be (　　　　　　　) at the library at around 3:00 tomorrow.
4. Paul is (　　　　　　　) in the river.
5. It is (　　　　　　　) in Hokkaido now.

B 各文の（　　　）内の動詞をかえて過去進行形、現在進行形、未来進行形の文を完成させましょう。

1. Beth and Steve (study) for the exam at the library.

    過去進行形　Beth and Steve _____ for the exam then.

    現在進行形　Beth and Steve _____ for the exam now.

    未来進行形　Beth and Steve _____ for the exam.

2. I (have) a good time.

    過去進行形　I _____ a good time.

    現在進行形　I _____ a good time.

    未来進行形　I _____ a good time.

C （　　）内の動詞を使って進行形の文を完成させましょう。

1. The dogs _____ a lot last night. (bark)
2. I _____ Professor Smith's class this semester. (take)
3. Please be quiet. My baby _____. (sleep)
4. A: I'm thirsty.

    B: You can get a drink at the vending machine over there.
    I _____ for you here. (wait)
5. I saw you at the cafeteria. You _____ sandwiches. (eat)

D 日本語の文に合うように適切な動詞を過去形、現在形、未来形、または進行形にして、（　　）に入れましょう。

1. スージーが今私のコンピュータを使っています。

    Suzie（　　　　　　　　）my computer now.
2. 私の兄は科学についてよく知っています。

    My brother（　　　　　　　　）a lot about science.
3. 私達は２時間前に家を出ました。

    We（　　　　　　　　）home two hours ago.
4. 明日は雨が降るでしょう。

    It（　　　　　　　　）tomorrow.
5. 彼らはレポートを書いていた。

    They（　　　　　　　　）a paper.

E ミュージックフェスティバルでの会話を読んで、問題に答えましょう。

Yusuke: Look, a lot of people are laughing and (a)(clap) their hands over there.

Sakura: Two clowns are (b)(juggle).

Yusuke: I will go and get a program at the information desk.

(He comes back with a program and they look at it.)

Yusuke: The country and western band Green Field is playing on Stage B, and hip-hop dancers are (c)(perform) on Stage C.

Sakura: Oh, we missed the Jefferson Trio. They are a very famous jazz band. I went to their concert last year and I really (d)(enjoy) it.

Yusuke: Well, they will play again at night, so we can (e)(listen) to them later.

Sakura: OK. Look, they are selling souvenirs over there. Let's go and buy a T-shirt first.

Yusuke: All right.

注) **clown** ピエロ　　**souvenir** 記念の品

1. （　　）内の動詞を適切な形に直しましょう
   (a) clap _____ (b) juggle _____
   (c) perform _____ (d) enjoy _____
   (e) listen _____

2. 祐介とさくらはミュージックフェスティバルで何をしようと思っていますか。日本語で２つ書きましょう。

   _____
   _____

Unit 7 受動態

> 受動態は、「〜される」と表現したい時に be 動詞 + 動詞の過去分詞で表します。

◇（　　）に適切な語句を書きましょう。

能動態　The children **like** him.　　　子供達は彼が好きです。
受動態　He **is liked** by the children.　彼は子供達に（　　　　　　　）

◇動詞の語形変化を完成させましょう。

原形	過去形	過去分詞形	意味
bring			
give			
grow			
hold			
know			
leave			
read			
choose			
see			
sell			
speak			
take			
write			

＊能動態の主語は受動態の文では by〜「〜に（よって）」で表しますが、必要ない文もよくあります。

Spanish is spoken in Chile.

A （　　）内の動詞をかえて過去形、現在形、未来形の受動態の文を完成させましょう。

> You (invite) to the party.

過去形　You _____ to the party.

現在形　You _____ to the party.

未来形　You _____ to the party.

B 次の文の中から、受動態の文をすべて選びましょう。

1. I will be back by noon.
2. The windows are open.
3. My brother was eating ice cream by the river.
4. Your plan will be accepted at the meeting.
5. The cake tasted good.
6. The book is read all over the world.

C 時制に注意しながら（　　）内の動詞を使って受動態の文を完成させましょう。

1. Graduation ceremonies (　　) (　　) in March in Japan. (hold)
2. A package (　　) (　　) (　　) tomorrow morning. (deliver)
3. A lot of things (　　) (　　) on the Internet these days. (sell)
4. *Romeo and Juliet* (　　) (　　) by William Shakespeare. (write)
5. Five people (　　) (　　) in the accident. (injure)

D 受動態、能動態のどちらなのかを考えながら、(　　) 内の動詞を使って文を完成させましょう。

1. The boy _____ to the hospital yesterday.　(take)
2. John's parents _____ him to the zoo last Sunday.　(take)
3. Strawberries can _____ in the greenhouse.　(pick)
4. I _____ some money on New Year's Day,　(give)

   so I bought a pair of shoes.
5. My aunt is going to leave her house at 9.　(arrive)

   She _____ here by 10.
6. The report must _____ on Wednesday.　(submit)

E 日本語の文に合うように語句を並びかえて英文を完成させ、全文を書きましょう。ただし、余分な語が1語含まれています。文頭の文字が小文字表記になっている場合があります。

1. その猫はその家族にタマと呼ばれています。
   [by / called / calling / is / the cat / the family / Tama].
   _____

2. 南十字星はオーストラリアで見ることができます。
   [Australia / be / can / in / see / seen / the Southern Cross].
   _____

F 友人についての文章と会話を読んで、問題に答えましょう。 CD 08

I have an old friend. Her name is Vicky. Vicky has a bad habit. Sometimes bad things happen because of her carelessness, but for her, they are never her fault. For example, yesterday we had this conversation:

Vicky: I made soup for dinner last night. The soup was left on the table, and it smells bad now. I have to throw it away. I'm so angry.
Me: Vicky, you live alone, so YOU left the soup out on the table.
Vicky: Well, that's true, but someone called me after dinner, and I forgot about the soup.
Me: You should just say, "<u>I left the soup on the table</u> and it went bad."

注) **habit** くせ　　　**fault** 過失　　　**throw away** 捨てる

1. 本文に合うように、(　　) に適切な語句を入れましょう。
   ビッキーは「私」の[ⓐ](　　　　　　　) です。彼女は、自分の不注意で悪いことが起きたときでも、[ⓑ](　　　　　　　) とは考えません。昨日も、スープのことで怒っていました。

2. 下線部を受動態にした文を本文中から見つけましょう。

   _____

3. 次の下線部をビッキーならどう言うでしょう。受動態に書きかえましょう。
   <u>I broke my sister's plate</u>, so she is angry.

   _____

Unit 8 時制（3） 現在完了形

> 現在完了形は過去の出来事と今とのつながりがある時に使い、
> have / has ＋動詞の過去分詞で表します。

I <u>came</u> here last year and I <u>am</u> still here. = I **have been** here since last year.
　過去　　　　　　　　　　　現在

＊現在完了の文は、副詞（語・句・節）や文脈等が解釈の手がかりになります。

◇次の英文を日本語に訳しましょう。

継続　I **have known** the family <u>for 6 years / since 2008</u>.

　　　私は6年間（6年前から）/ 2008年から＿＿＿＿＿＿＿＿＿＿＿＿＿＿＿＿

経験　I **have** <u>never</u> **swum** in the sea.

　　　＿＿＿＿＿＿＿＿＿＿＿＿＿＿＿＿＿＿＿＿＿＿＿＿＿＿＿＿＿＿＿＿＿

完了　We **have** <u>already</u> **finished** dinner.

　　　＿＿＿＿＿＿＿＿＿＿＿＿＿＿＿＿＿＿＿＿＿＿＿＿＿＿＿＿＿＿＿＿＿

結果　A: What's wrong?
　　　B: I **have lost** my smartphone.

　　　＿＿＿＿＿＿＿＿＿＿＿＿＿＿＿＿＿＿＿＿＿＿＿＿＿＿＿＿＿＿＿＿＿

＊副詞が過去の一時点を表す語句（last summer, yesterday, 3 days ago, in 2010など）のみの場合、動詞は過去形になります。

　　◇（　　　）にbe動詞の過去形か現在完了形を入れましょう。
　1　I（　　　　　）busy <u>last week</u>.
　2　I（　　　　　）busy <u>since last week</u>.

Ⓐ 現在完了形の文をすべて選びましょう。

1. Swahili is spoken in Kenya.
2. We have just eaten dinner.
3. My mother has a tired face.
4. Michael is looking for a job.
5. The teacher has read all the essays.

Ⓑ (　　) の動詞を使って現在完了形の文を完成させましょう。

1. I (　　) (　　) him since we were in high school. (love)
2. Andy (　　) already (　　) to school. (come)
3. The sun (　　) just (　　). (rise)
4. Someone (　　) (　　) the door open. (leave)
5. I (　　) (　　) the article before. (read)
6. The students (　　) (　　) three tests this month. (take)
7. Mr. Newman (　　) (　　) at least 10 books. (write)
8. She (　　) (　　) Mt. Fuji many times. (climb)
9. My mother (　　) never (　　) the dishes. (do)
10. My uncle and aunt (　　) (　　) in Australia since 1993. (live)

C ( ) 内から適切な語句を選びましょう。

1. The package (arrived, has arrived) three days ago.
2. My mother (was, has been) busy since last Monday.
3. The TV program (starts, has started) at 8 a.m.
4. Lily (will go, has gone) to America. I miss her a lot.

D 日本語の文に合うように語句を並びかえて英文を完成させ、全文を書きましょう。ただし、余分な語が1語含まれています。文頭の文字が小文字表記になっている場合があります。

1. 私達の先生は外国に行った事はありませんが、英語をとても流暢に話します。
   [a foreign country / been / has / never / our teacher / to / went], but he speaks English very fluently.

   _____

2. 私は2010年から田中さんに3回会っています。
   I [for / have / Mr. Tanaka / seen / since / three times / 2010].

   _____

3. 私は本をもう図書館に返却しました。
   [returned / have already / I / the book / the library / to / yet].

   _____

4. 彼は一週間前から病気です。
   [a / ago / been / for / has / he / sick] week.

   _____

E to-do list（するべきことのリスト）についての文章を読んで、問題に答えましょう。

I live with my cousin, Yuka. We became roommates 2 months ago. We invited some of our friends for lunch at noon today. We have 4 things on our to-do list.

☐ Clean the living room
☐ Clean the bathroom
☐ Go to the supermarket and buy soft drinks
☐ Cook lunch

It is 11 o'clock now. I cleaned the living room after breakfast. Yuka has been in the kitchen since 9:00. She is still cooking. She is a very good cook. She has cooked roast chicken for me several times. I've just come back from the supermarket. I have to put the drinks into the refrigerator first. Then, I'm going to clean the bathroom. After that, I'll help Yuka.

注）refrigerator　冷蔵庫

1. 本文に合うように、（　　）に適切な語を入れて現在完了形の文を作りましょう。
   a. I (　　　　) (　　　　　) Yuka's roast chicken.
   b. We have (　　　　) roommates (　　　　　) 2 months.

2. 「私」と由香がすでに済ませたことは何ですか。本文中の□にチェック（✓）を入れましょう。

3. 次の質問に日本語で答えましょう。
   a. 今、由香は何をしていますか。＿＿＿＿＿＿＿＿＿＿＿＿＿＿＿
   b. 今から「私」は何をしますか。＿＿＿＿＿＿＿＿＿＿＿＿＿＿＿
   c. 今から友達が来るまでどのくらい時間がありますか。
   ＿＿＿＿＿＿＿＿＿＿＿＿＿＿＿＿＿＿＿＿＿＿＿＿＿＿＿＿＿

Unit 9 否定文

> 否定文の作り方には、述語動詞の最初の語の後ろに not を入れる場合と、述語動詞の前に do not・does not・did not を持ってきて述語動詞は原形にする場合の2通りあります。

◇（　　）に適切な語句を入れて、否定文を作りましょう。

1 述語動詞の最初の語の後ろに not を入れる。

	肯定文	否定文
be 動詞	Scott **is able to run** fast.	Scott (　　　　　　　　) fast.
	I **was invited** to the party.	I (　　　　　　　　) to the party.
助動詞	Mari **will cook** tomorrow.	Mari (　　　　　　　　) tomorrow.
	You **must be** here.	You (　　　　　　　　) here.
現在完了	We **have eaten** lunch.	We (　　　　　　　　) lunch.

2 述語動詞の前に do not・does not・did not を持ってきて、述語動詞は原形にする。

	肯定文	否定文
一般動詞（現在形）	I **have** a cold.	I (　　　　　　　　) a cold.
	Lisa **knows** my wife.	Lisa (　　　　　　　　) my wife.
一般動詞（過去形）	I **went** to work.	I (　　　　　　　　) to work.
have to	The boy **has to** take the test.	The boy (　　　　　　　　) the test.

＊ must と have to はどちらも「〜しなければならない」という意味ですが、否定文にすると意味が変わります。

◇次の英文を日本語に訳しましょう。
You **mustn't** stay here. ＿＿＿＿＿＿＿＿＿＿＿＿＿＿＿＿＿＿
You **don't have to** stay here. ＿＿＿＿＿＿＿＿＿＿＿＿＿＿＿＿＿＿

A 文を否定文にしましょう。

1. The students are in the gym.   → The students _____ in the gym.
2. He has told me the news.   → He _____ me the news.
3. The man was wearing a tie.   → The man _____ a tie.
4. My brother and I live together.   → My brother and I _____ together.
5. I tried a spicy soup in Nepal.   → I _____ a spicy soup in Nepal.
6. We have to work on Saturday.   → We _____ on Saturday.

B 文を否定文にしましょう。

1. a. Fred built the house.   →_____
   b. The house was built by Fred.   →_____
2. a. Jack is a fast runner.   →_____
   b. Jack runs fast.   →_____
   c. Jack can run fast.   →_____
   d. Jack is able to run fast.   →_____
3. a. He will find a good job.   →_____
   b. He is going to find a good job.   →_____

C 英文を日本語に訳しましょう。

1. You mustn't eat or drink in the computer room.

_____

2. We have a lot of food in the refrigerator, so we don't have to go to the supermarket today.

_____

D リストから適語を選んで（　　　）に入れましょう。同じ語を繰り返し使う事はできません。

> isn't　　wasn't　　haven't　　doesn't　　didn't

1. I (　　　　) eat breakfast this morning.
2. Rachel (　　　　　) sleeping at that time.
3. This class (　　　　　) make me sleepy.
4. My parents (　　　　　) been to Germany.
5. The perfume (　　　　　) sold in Japan.

E 日本語の文に合うように語句を並びかえて英文を完成させましょう。文頭の文字が小文字表記になっている場合があります。

1. その地域は安全ではない。だから、1人でそこに行くべきではない。
   [go / is / not / not / safe / should / the area / there / you]
   _____, so _____ alone.

2. ソフィーはあまりお金を持っていないが、心配はしていない。
   [does / have / is / Sophie / much money / not / not / she / worried]
   _____, but _____.

F ある兄弟姉妹についての文章を読んで、問題に答えましょう。 CD 10

There are six people in my family: my parents and four children. My sister Donna didn't have any brothers or sisters for the first four years of her life. Then I was born. I wasn't the first child for my parents, but I wasn't the last, either. Three years later, twin sisters were born, and I became a big brother.

I still live with my parents. I am not sure yet, but I may leave home next year. Donna moved out last year and ⓐshe lives alone now. The twins are still 15, so ⓑthey will stay at home for at least another three years.

注）**either** （否定文で）〜も　　　**move out** 引っ越す　　　**at least** 少なくとも

1. 下線部と同じ意味になるように（　　）に適切な語を入れましょう。

    ⓐ She (　　　　) live with us any more.

    ⓑ The twins are 15, and they (　　　　) (　　　　) leave home for at least another three years.

2. 次の質問に答えましょう。

    a. 私には何人の兄弟姉妹がいますか。
       兄弟：_____　　　　姉妹：_____
    b. 私とドナはそれぞれ何歳ですか。
       私：_____　　　　ドナ：_____
    c. 今この家には何人の人が住んでいますか。_____

Unit 10 疑問文

> Yes/No 疑問文の作り方には、述語動詞の最初の語を主語の前に持ってくる場合と、主語の前に do・does・did を置いて、述語動詞を原形にする場合の2通りあります。

◇（　　　）に適切な語句を入れて、疑問文と答えを作りましょう。

1　述語動詞の最初の語を主語の前に持ってくる。

	肯定文	疑問文	答え
be 動詞	You **are** Greg.	(　　) you Greg?	Yes, (　　) (　　). No, (　　) (　　).
助動詞	I **can sit** here.	(　　) I (　　) here?	Yes, (　　) (　　). No, (　　) (　　).
現在完了形	She **has arrived**.	(　　) she (　　　)?	Yes, (　　) (　　). No, (　　)(　　).

2　主語の前に do・does・did を置いて、述語動詞を原形にする。

	肯定文	疑問文	答え
一般動詞 （現在形）	They **leave** home at 8.	(　　) they (　　) home at 8?	Yes, (　　) (　　). No, (　　) (　　).
一般動詞 （過去形）	Joe **ate** lunch.	(　　) Joe (　　) lunch?	Yes, (　　) (　　). No, (　　) (　　).

＊疑問詞を使った疑問文は基本的に Yes/No 疑問文の前に疑問詞を置いて作ります。
　The book was written <u>in 2000</u>.　→　Was the book written <u>in 2000</u>?
　　　　　　　　　　　　　　　　　　　　When was the book written?

＊「疑問詞＋名詞」で使われるものもあります。
　1. **Whose book** is this?　　これは誰の本ですか。
　2. **What color** do you like?　あなたは何色が好きですか。

A 各文をYes/No疑問文にしましょう。

1. The windows were broken 2 days ago.
   _____

2. He visits his sick mother every Saturday.
   _____

3. The students have to clean their classroom after school.
   _____

4. Lucy read the book at the library.
   _____

5. Sharon has been in Sendai for a year.
   _____

6. The band will be popular soon.
   _____

B リストから疑問詞を選び、下線部を問う疑問文を完成させましょう。ただし、余分な語句が含まれています。

```
who     whose     what     how     how many
how much     what time
```

1. You leave home <u>at 8</u> every day.   (   ) do you leave home every day?
2. Carl ate <u>pasta</u> for dinner.   (   ) did Carl eat for dinner?
3. Ann bought <u>three</u> shirts.   (   ) shirts did Ann buy?
4. She comes to school <u>by bus</u>.   (   ) does she come to school?
5. These are <u>my</u> gloves.   (   ) gloves are these?

C 下線部を問う疑問文を作りましょう。

1. They are going to the department store.
   _____

2. He broke the window last Wednesday.
   _____

3. Your sister has known the man for 7 years.
   _____

4. Their father plays tennis.
   _____

D 対話文の（　）に適切な語を入れましょう。

1. A: (　　　) (　　　) Kate (　　　) on weekends?
   B: She goes out with her friends.

2. A: (　　　) (　　　) the cat (　　　)?
   B: It's called Mii.

3. A: (　　　) (　　　) (　　　) absent yesterday?
   B: I was sick.

4. A: (　　　) (　　　) you see Rie?
   B: At the shopping mall. She was with her friends.

5. A: (　　　) you finished your homework yet?
   B: (　　　), I (　　　). It was very easy.

6. A: (　　　) I open the present now?
   B: (　　　), you (　　　) (　　　). You have to wait.

E あるゲームについての文章を読んで、下の問題に答えましょう。

　　Twenty Questions is a popular game in America. People play it around the dinner table or in the car on a trip. One person thinks of a person, place or thing, and the other people ask questions and guess the answer. The questions must be yes-no questions.

A: OK, I'm ready.
　　It is a thing.
B: Can I eat it?
A: No, you can't.
B: Do I use it at school?
A: Yes, you do.
B: Have we seen it today?
A: Yes, we have.
B: Is it in this room?
A: Yes, it is.
B: Does it have four legs?
A: Yes, it does.
B: Is it a chair?
A: No, it isn't.
B: _____?
A: Yes, you got it.

注) **guess** 〜を推測する

1. 下線部に適切な疑問文を入れましょう。

_____

2. 3〜4人グループになって、Twenty Questions をやってみましょう。最初に person, place, thing のうちどれを選んだか言ってからゲームを始めましょう。

Unit 11 比較級・最上級

> 形容詞、副詞の形を変えることによって、2つ以上のものを比べることができます。

比較級・最上級の作り方

		原級	比較級	最上級
1	比較的短い語の場合	small	smaller	smallest
2	比較的長い語の場合	interesting	more interesting	most interesting
3	不規則変化をする語	good/well	better	best
		bad	worse	worst
		many/much	more	most

◇次の英文を日本語に訳しましょう。

1. 2つのものを比べて同じぐらいの時　　**as** 原級 **as**
   Tim is **as** tall **as** his father.　　ティムはお父さんと同じぐらいの背丈だ。
   Tim isn't **as** tall **as** his brother.　　_____

2. 2つのものを比べて違いがある時　　**-er** あるいは **more** ～
   Tim runs fast**er than** Jerry.　　ティムはジェリーより速く走る。
   Tim's car is **more** expensive **than** this truck.　　_____

3. 3つ以上のものの中で一番～と言う時　　**the -est** あるいは **the most** ～
   Tim is **the** young**est** of the three.　　ティムは3人の中で一番若い。
   Tim talks **(the) mos**t quickly of all his brothers._____

＊比較の表現には次のようなものがあります。

　　◇英文を日本語に訳しましょう。
　　・**as ～ as possible**　　できるだけ～
　　　Tim ran **as** fast **as possible**.　　_____

文の間違いを正して全文を書き直しましょう。

1. Today will be more hotter than yesterday.

2. Tokyo Tower isn't as taller as Tokyo Sky Tree.

3. I can speak Spanish the wellest in my class.

4. I'm going to study more hard than you.

5. This guidebook was useful than the website.

B （　　）内の語を比較級か最上級にかえて文を完成させ、全文を日本語に訳しましょう。

1. She looks _____ this year than last year. (healthy)

2. You are late again. You should get up _____. (early)

3. She is dancing _____ of all the girls. (well)

4. We have stayed in the _____ hotel in Madrid. (popular)

5. It rains _____ in Matsue than in my hometown. (often)

6. Roy has read _____ books than Helen. (many)

C 日本語の文に合うように語句を並びかえて英文を完成させ、全文を書きましょう。文頭の文字が小文字表記になっている場合があります。

1. 私はいつもほど上手に歌うことができなかった。
   [able / as / as usual / I / sing / to / wasn't / well].
   _____

2. あなたは出来るだけ早くその仕事を辞めるべきだ。
   [as / as / the job / possible / quit / should / soon / you].
   _____

D 各組の最初の文と同じ内容になるように、(　　) に適切な語を入れましょう。

1. Taro ate 2 hamburgers. Jiro ate 5 hamburgers.

   Jiro ate (　　　　) hamburgers than Taro.

   Taro (　　　　) eat as (　　　　) hamburgers (　　　　) Jiro.

2. Kei is 21 years old. Ren is 24 years old. Jen is 18 years old.

   Jen is (　　　) (　　　) Kei.

   Kei is (　　　) (　　　) (　　　) as Ren.

   Ren is the (　　　) of the three.

E big, small のいずれかを選び適切な形にかえて比較の文を作りましょう。

1. Australia is _____ continent.
2. Greenland is _____ island.
3. Canada is _____ China.
4. Australia is _____ Brazil.
5. Japan isn't _____ as Thailand.

F 惑星に関する文章を読んで、問題に答えましょう。

Our solar system has eight planets. They are Mercury, Venus, Earth, Mars, Jupiter, Saturn, Uranus and Neptune. They all travel around the sun. Mercury is the nearest to the sun. Neptune is the farthest away and it takes about 165 years to travel around the sun!

How many moons does Earth have? Yes, just one and it is the moon. Saturn has the most moons of all the planets. Mercury and Venus don't have any moons.

Let's compare the sizes of Earth, Jupiter, Neptune, Saturn and Uranus. The biggest planet is Jupiter. ⓐUnderline: Uranus is not as big as Saturn. ⓑUnderline: Neptune is smaller than Uranus. ⓒUnderline: Earth is smaller than the other four planets.

注）solar system　太陽系　　　compare　〜を比較する

1. 本文の内容に合うように、（　　　）に適切な語を入れましょう。
   a. Saturn has (　　　　　) moons than Earth.
   b. Jupiter isn't as (　　　　　) from the sun as Neptune.

2. 下線部を指示に従って書きかえましょう。
   ⓐ　Saturn を主語にして比較級に

   ⓑ　Uranus を主語にして as 〜 as を使って

   ⓒ　最上級に

3. Earth, Jupiter, Neptune, Saturn, Uranus を大きい順に並べましょう。
   ＿＿＿＿＿ → ＿＿＿＿＿ → ＿＿＿＿＿ → ＿＿＿＿＿ → ＿＿＿＿＿

Unit 12 副詞の働きをする（1）前置詞＋名詞

> 「前置詞＋名詞」のように主語と述語動詞を持たない語の集まりを句と言います。「前置詞＋名詞」には副詞と同様に、動詞・文を修飾する働きがあります。

◇（　　　）に修飾部の意味を書きましょう。

副詞　　　　　We cooked dinner together.

　　　　　　　私たちは（　　　　　　　）夕食を作った。

前置詞＋名詞　We cooked dinner with our friends.

　　　　　　　私たちは（　　　　　　　）夕食を作った。

＊前置詞には after, for, in, to, on などがあります。

　◇（　　　）に適切な前置詞を入れましょう。

　We cooked dinner (　　　　) the lawn.　　（芝生の上で）

　We cooked dinner (　　　　) the sunset.　（日没後に）

　We cooked dinner (　　　　) our parents.　（両親のために）

＊「前置詞＋名詞」をいくつか一緒に使うこともできます。

　◇次の英文を日本語に訳しましょう。

　We cooked dinner with our children in the backyard in summer.

　──────────────────────────

A 日本語に合うように、(　　) に適切な前置詞を入れましょう。また、(　　) ＋名詞部分を隠して、日本語訳の助けを借りながら全文をすらすら言えるように何回も音読しましょう。

時を表す前置詞

1. I came home (　　) 4:30.
   4時半に
2. I visit my grandparents (　　) summer/August.
   夏に／八月に
3. I have four classes (　　) Monday.
   月曜日に
4. I'll be here (　　) 7:30.
   7時半まで
5. I have to finish my homework (　　) Friday.
   金曜日までに
6. He's going to get a driver's license (　　) the summer vacation.
   夏休みの間に
7. I usually sleep (　　) 7 hours.
   7時間
8. The shop is opened (　　) 9 (　　) 6.
   9時から6時まで

場所を表す前置詞

1. I left my umbrella (　　) the bus stop.
   バス停で
2. She always has candy (　　) her bag.
   カバンの中に
3. You can put your bag (　　) the sofa.
   ソファーの上に
4. I live (　　) Kyoto.
   京都の近くに
5. The train runs (　　) the river.
   川に沿って

6. Eight planets travel ( ) the sun.
　　　　　太陽の周りを
7. I always walk ( ) the station.
　　　　　　　駅へ
8. The boy hid ( ) the curtain.
　　　　カーテンの後ろに
9. Tadashi is sitting ( ) Rina and Haruka.
　　　　里奈と春香の間に
10. They live ( ) us.
　　　　私達の上（の階）に
11. I had to speak ( ) a lot of people.
　　　　たくさんの人の前で

その他の前置詞

1. We cut vegetables ( ) a knife.
　　　　ナイフで
2. I did my work ( ) any help.
　　　　助けなしで
3. My brother works there ( ) a waiter.
　　　　ウェイターとして
4. The baby walks ( ) a penguin.
　　　　ペンギンのように
5. The actor is very popular ( ) young Asian people.
　　　　アジアの若者たちの間で
6. I danced ( ) a white dress.
　　　　白いドレスを着て
7. The building was designed ( ) Antonio Gaudi.
　　　　アントニオ・ガウディによって

B a certain fruit（ある果物）を使ったレシピを読んで、問題に答えましょう。

🎧 13

　I love this dish and I cook it for breakfast on the weekend. Here is the recipe.

　First, mix some flour, one egg and some milk in a bowl. Then, mash a certain fruit and mix it up with the mixture. Then, heat a frying pan and put butter in it. Pour the mixture into it and cook it for a while. Next, turn it over and cook it for one minute. Now, put it on a plate. Put some butter and some maple syrup on it. Honey, jam or sugar is also fine. Finally, you can eat it.

　What is this dish called?

注) **flour**　小麦粉　　　　**mash**　〜をすりつぶす　　　　**pour**　〜を注ぐ
　　for a while　しばらくの間

1. 副詞の働きをする「前置詞＋（代）名詞」を○で囲み、修飾される動詞に下線を引きましょう。

2. a certain fruit は何か考えて、下線にアルファベットを書き入れてこの料理名を完成させましょう。

　　___ a ___ a ___ a　　___ a ___ ___ a ___ ___

3. 次の絵を作り方順に並べかえましょう。ただし、余分な絵が1つ含まれています。

　　　　a　　　　　b　　　　　c　　　　　d　　　　　e

_____ → _____ → _____ → _____

Unit 13 副詞の働きをする（2）to 不定詞

> to 不定詞には動詞・文を修飾する副詞の働きがあり、目的や理由などを表します。to 不定詞は to ＋動詞の原形で作ります。

◇次の文の間違いを直しましょう。

I got up early to doing my homework.

I turned on the computer to wrote an e-mail.

* to 不定詞は感情を表す形容詞とともに使われ、その感情の理由を説明することもあります。

◇（　　　）に修飾部の意味を書きましょう。

I <u>went</u> to America to study English .

私は（　　　　　　　）アメリカに行きました。

We <u>were surprised</u> to see you there .

私たちは（　　　　　　　）驚きました。

* to 不定詞を使った構文には次のようなものがあります。

◇英文を日本語に訳しましょう。

・too … to ～　　～するのに…過ぎる、…過ぎて～できない

I was **too** busy **to** take a bath.

・… enough to ～　　～するのに（十分）…だ

He is old **enough to** drive a car.

文の続きとして最も適切なものをリストから選び文を完成させ、全文を日本語に訳しましょう。同じ語句を繰り返し使う事はできません。

> to tell her the good news
> to see the accident in front of my house
> to celebrate my birthday
> to keep in shape
> to surprise him

1. My parents took me to a restaurant _____.

2. He jogs and swims every day _____.

3. I called Mary _____.

4. I painted my brother's bicycle pink _____.

5. I was shocked _____.

B 英文中に to が必要な場所に ∧ を入れて、日本語に訳しましょう。

1. He stood up hand me a newspaper.

2. She was excited get a ticket for the play.

3. My sister was too tired go out for dinner tonight.

C 日本語の文に合うように語句を並びかえて英文を完成させ、全文を書きましょう。文頭の文字が小文字表記になっている場合があります。

1. 多くの人々が異文化を体験するために外国を訪れる。
   [countries / people / different cultures / experience / foreign / many / to / visit].

2. その女性は親切にも私を博物館に連れて行ってくれました。
   [enough / kind / me / take / to the museum / the woman / to / was].

D 日本語の文に合うように、(　　　) に適切な語を入れましょう。

1. ジャンさんは私達に中国語を教えるために日本に来ました。
   Mr. Jiang came to Japan (　　　) (　　　) (　　　) (　　　).
2. 彼はお風呂に入るために服を脱いだ。
   He took off his clothes (　　　) (　　　) (　　　) (　　　).
3. 遅れてすみません。
   I am sorry (　　　) (　　　) (　　　).

E コーラについての文章を読んで、問題に答えましょう。

You all know cola, right? We can buy it at various places such as convenience stores and vending machines. We may enjoy this soft drink on a hot summer day to feel refreshed. However, in the 19th century, people drank it for a different reason. In those days, they drank it to help digestion. It was a kind of medicine. So they went to a drug store to buy cola.

The name "cola" comes from a plant. In the old days, they used nuts of cola plants to make cola drinks. Cola nuts aren't usually used any more, but the name has survived to this day.

注) digestion　消化

1. 副詞の働きをする to 不定詞の句を○で囲み、修飾される動詞に下線を引きましょう。

2. 本文に合うように、a〜e をうめて表を完成させましょう。

	昔	今
コーラを飲む理由	a	b
コーラを買う場所	c	d
e	コーラを作るのに使われていた。	コーラを作るのにあまり使われない。

Unit 14 副詞の働きをする（3）接続詞＋節

「接続詞＋節」には、動詞・節を修飾する副詞の働きをするものがあります。節とは主語と述語動詞を持った語の集まりを言います。

◇（　　　）に修飾部の意味を書きましょう。

He smiled **when** he saw me.　　彼は（　　　　　　　　）ほほ笑んだ。

I will call you **if** I finish early.　　私は（　　　　　　　　）あなたにお電話します。

＊副詞の働きをする節（副詞節）は、文頭にもってくることもできます。その時は副詞節の最後にコンマが必要です。
　If I finish early, I will call you.

「副詞の働きをする語・句・節」のまとめ

◇（　　　）に修飾部の意味を書きましょう。

副詞　　　　I studied English **yesterday**.
　　　　　　私は（　　　　　　　　）英語を勉強した。

前置詞＋名詞　I studied English **for the test**.
　　　　　　私は（　　　　　　　　）英語を勉強した。

to 不定詞　　I studied English **to pass** the test.
　　　　　　私は（　　　　　　　　）英語を勉強した。

接続詞＋節　I studied English **because I had a test**.
　　　　　　私は（　　　　　　　　）英語を勉強した。

A 副詞節を○で囲み、全文を日本語に訳しましょう。

1. I usually brush my teeth after I eat breakfast.

2. Olivia majored in psychology because she was interested in people.

3. Tomo's old friends came while he was out.

4. We were watching TV when our father came home.

B （　）に入る接続詞をリストの中から選び、全文を日本語に訳しましょう。同じ語を繰り返し使う事はできません。

because　until　if　although

1. I was late for the class (　　　　) I missed the train.

2. Please ask me (　　　　) you have a question.

3. (　　　　) I work very hard, I don't have much money in my bank account.

4. Wait (　　　　) I call you.

C 次の3つの接続詞と4つの節を自由に組み合わせて文を作りましょう。

接続詞

though   as   after

節

I went jogging   I went to bed early
I did my homework   I was sick

例）I went jogging after I did my homework.

1. _____
2. _____
3. _____

D リストにある接続詞を使って、自由に英文を完成させましょう。

before   after   because   though

例）The students stood up <u>when their teacher came in</u>.

1. Natsuki takes a bath _____
2. We call the dog Kuro _____

E 招待状と4人の友人の出欠の返事を読んで、問題に答えましょう。

Please join us at Sylvie's 21st Birthday Party

Date   October 11th
Time   17:30-21:00
Location   Sylvie's House
Address   85 Lincoln Street

Call Bill by October 5th at 555-1234

Beth "I'll be there at 6, but (a)(   ) I have an exam the next day, I'm going to leave at 8."

Paul "I'll be an hour late because I have to work until 6. But I can stay until the end of the party."

Sam "I can come one hour earlier to help you. I can also stay and clean up the house (b)(   ) everyone leaves."

Chris "I'm sorry, but I have to work from 7 on that day. I'll drop by 10 minutes before 7 to bring her a birthday present (c)(   ) I can't stay."

注）**drop by** 立ち寄る

1. リストから最も適切な語を選び（　　　）に入れましょう。同じ語を繰り返し使う事はできません。

   although   after   because

2. 次の質問に答えましょう。

   a. パーティ当日、シルビーの家に来る順に名前を挙げましょう。
   _____ → _____ → _____ → _____

   b. パーティ当日、シルビーの家から帰る順に名前を挙げましょう。
   _____ → _____ → _____ → _____

Unit 15 形容詞の働きをする（1）前置詞＋名詞

「前置詞＋名詞」には名詞を修飾する形容詞の働きもあります。その場合は修飾される名詞の後に置きます。

◇次の語句を日本語に訳しましょう。

a dog **with** long ears　　　　　長い耳をもつ　　　　　_____

the shop **next to** my house　　　_____　　　_____

the bicycle **below** the window　_____　　　_____

＊これらの前置詞句は文中で次のように使われます。

I have a dog **with long ears**.

The shop **next to my house** is open until 11.

The bicycle **below the window** is very old.

「前置詞＋名詞」のまとめ

◇（　　　）に適切な語句を入れましょう。

副詞の働き　　The boy is sitting **behind Brenda**.

　　　　　　　その少年は（　　　　　　　　　）座っています。

形容詞の働き　The boy **behind Brenda** is Max.

　　　　　　　（　　　　　　　　　）少年はマックスです。

A 日本語の文に合うように、（　）内の語句を入れて英文を完成させましょう。

1. サッカーは世界中の人々に愛されています。
   Soccer is loved by people.　　　　　　（around the world）
   _____

2. ベッドの下の箱は空です。
   The boxes are empty.　　　　　　（under the bed）
   _____

3. チャールズはその棚の本を全部読んだ。
   Charles has read all the books.　　　　　　（on the shelf）
   _____

4. ウィルソン氏による最終的な決断は驚くべきものだった。
   The final decision was surprising.　　　　　　（by Mr. Wilson）
   _____

B 日本語の文に合うように、リストから適切な前置詞を選んで（　）に入れましょう。ただし、余分な語が含まれています。

> across　　along　　for　　in　　on　　with

1. 私は通りの向こう側の薬局によく行きます。
   I often go to the pharmacy (　　　　) the street.

2. 私の叔父は、ガーデニングが好きなので大きな庭の付いた家が欲しい。
   My uncle wants a house (　　　　) a big garden because he loves gardening.

3. リムさんは私にピアノリサイタルの為のドレスを見せてくれた。
   Ms. Lim showed me the dress (　　　　) her piano recital.

4. トンプソンさんは日本のポップカルチャーについての本を買うつもりだ。
   Ms. Thompson is going to buy a book (　　　　) Japanese pop culture.

C 英文を日本語に訳しましょう。また、下線部の働きが形容詞的、副詞的のどちらかを考えて○をつけましょう。

1. Cherry trees were planted <u>around the pond</u>.　　　形容詞的／副詞的

2. The cherry trees <u>around the pond</u> were planted by my father.
　　　形容詞的／副詞的

3. Please put the coat <u>on the sofa</u>.　　　形容詞的／副詞的

4. Please give me the coat <u>on the sofa</u>.　　　形容詞的／副詞的

D 日本語の文に合うように語句を並びかえて英文を完成させ、全文を書きましょう。文頭の文字が小文字表記になっている場合があります。

1. その本の表紙は私の美術の先生によってデザインされました。
[art teacher / by / designed / my / of / the cover / the book / was].

2. 青いシャツを着た女の子は、夏休みにいとこに会いにカナダに行った。
[the blue shirt / Canada / during the summer vacation / in / the girl / to / went] to see her cousin.

3. 彼のような慎重な学生でも、そのような間違いを犯すことがあります。
Even [a / can / careful / him / like / make / student / such a mistake].

E 図形を見ながら文章を読んで、問題に答えましょう。 🎧 16

(1) The square between the two lines is grey. It is also between the two triangles. The line above the square is black. The square next to the circle is ⓐ_____.

(2) The line above the square is grey. The triangle next to the square is white. The black circle is next to the grey line. The line below the square is ⓑ_____.

(3) The square below the line is grey. The circle on the line is white. The other circle is below the line and it is black. The triangle at the bottom is white. The square above the line is ⓒ_____.

注) **above** 〜の上の

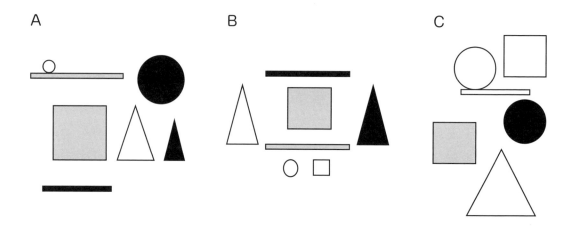

A　　　　　　　　　　B　　　　　　　　　　C

1. 形容詞の働きをする「前置詞＋名詞」を○で囲み、修飾される名詞に下線を引きましょう。

2. (1)〜(3)の文に合う絵を A〜C から選びましょう。
   (1) _____　(2) _____　(3) _____

3. 文中の下線部に色を表す英単語を書き入れましょう。

Unit 16 形容詞の働きをする（2）分詞

進行形で使われる現在分詞と受動態で使われる過去分詞には形容詞と同じ働きがあります。現在分詞は「〜している」、過去分詞は「〜された」と訳します。

◇下の □ と下線に日本語で意味を書きましょう。

A

The sweater is expensive. → the **expensive** sweater　　高価な　_____

The dog is barking. → the **barking** dog　　_____　_____

The car was stolen. → the **stolen** car　　_____　_____

B

The girl is kind to everyone. → the girl **kind** to everyone
　　　　　　　　　　　　　　　　みんなに優しい　女の子

The woman is walking with a dog. → the woman **walking** with a dog
　　　　　　　　　　　　　　　　_____　_____

The teacher is liked by everyone. → the teacher **liked** by everyone
　　　　　　　　　　　　　　　　_____　_____

＊名詞と分詞を含む形容詞句は文中で次のように使われます。

　The **stolen** car was found near the park yesterday.

　My brother knows the woman **walking with a dog**.

＊形容詞句は単独か修飾句を伴っているかによって置かれる場所が変わります。

　◇下線部に適切な語句を書きましょう。

　A：形容詞句が_____の時 → 名詞の前に置く。

　B：形容詞句が_____の時 → 名詞の後ろに置く。

日本語に合うように正しい方を○で囲みましょう。

1. a (breaking / broken) bicycle　　　　壊れた自転車
2. (dancing / danced) girls　　　　　　　踊っている女の子たち
3. (speaking / spoken) English　　　　　口語英語
4. the (wanting / wanted) man　　　　　指名手配中の男
5. a (sleeping / slept) cat　　　　　　　　眠っている猫

 リストから形容詞句を選び、適切な場所に入れて文を完成させましょう。同じ語句を繰り返し使う事はできません。

> walking with her hands in her pockets
> rising
> written by my father
> taken by Robert Capa during World War II

1. The book has a lot of illustrations.
   _____

2. The woman looks tired.
   _____

3. The children saw the sun with their parents.
   _____

4. The photograph is hanging on the wall.
   _____

C　現在分詞か過去分詞を含む形容詞句を○で囲み、修飾される名詞に下線を引きましょう。さらに全文を日本語に訳しましょう。

1. The flying bird looks like an airplane.

2. I've never eaten boiled eggs.

3. The table bought by the customer was made in Italy.

4. Ted was shocked to get a present wrapped in a newspaper from his girlfriend.

5. The girl doing the best in class will get the job.

D　日本語の文に合うように語句を並びかえて英文を完成させ、全文を書きましょう。文頭の文字が小文字表記になっている場合があります。

1. 向こうで花を植えている男性は私の誕生日にバラをくれた。
   [a rose / flowers / gave / me / over there / planting / the man] for my birthday.

2. 私達はお金を節約するために、中古車を買った。
   We [a / bought / car / money / save / to / used].

E 公園にいる人たちの様子を表す文章を読んで、問題に答えましょう。 🎧 17

  Mary is the woman sitting under the tree. She is talking with her sister's son, Tom. The girl looking at the singing bird is Jane. She is Mary's daughter. The boy walking a dog is her brother, Sam. The can kicked by Sam hits the woman wearing glasses. She is Mary's sister, Jill. She is sitting next to her husband, Larry. He is reading a book written by a popular Canadian writer.

  Kate and Sue are good friends of Mary's. Kate is drinking lemonade made by Mary. Sue is waving at the man with a broken leg. He is her husband, Bob. He was hit by a motorcycle three days ago.

1. 現在分詞と過去分詞を含む形容詞句を○で囲み、修飾される名詞に下線を引きましょう。

2. 絵の中に名前を書きましょう。

3. リストから適切な語を選んで（　　　）に入れましょう。ただし、余分な語が含まれています。

aunt	brother	cousin	daughter	husband
mother	sister	son	uncle	wife

 a. Jane is Mary's (　　　　).　　b. Sam is Mary's (　　　　).
 c. Larry is Jill's (　　　　).　　d. Tom is Sam's (　　　　).
 e. Mary is Jill's (　　　　).　　f. Sue is Bob's (　　　　).

Unit 17 形容詞の働きをする（3）to 不定詞

> to 不定詞には名詞を修飾する形容詞の働きがあります。その場合、to 不定詞は必ず名詞の後に持ってきます。

Kyoto has many places **to visit**. 京都には訪れるべき所がたくさんあります。

「to 不定詞」のまとめ

◇（　　　）に適切な語句を入れましょう。

副詞の働き　　Meg came from England **to teach** us yoga.
　　　　　　メグは（　　　　　　　　　　　）イングランドから来ました。

形容詞の働き　I found a person **to teach** us yoga.
　　　　　　私は（　　　　　　　　　　　）人を見つけました。

「形容詞の働きをする語句」のまとめ

◇（　　　）に修飾部の意味を書きましょう。

前置詞＋名詞	a woman **on** the stage	（　　　　　）女性
現在分詞	a woman **singing** a song	（　　　　　）女性
過去分詞	a woman **known** to everybody	（　　　　　）女性
to 不定詞	a woman **to do** the job	（　　　　　）女性

A 日本語の文に合うように、(　　　)内の語句を入れて英文を完成させましょう。

1. その仕事を最初にし終えた人はジェシカでした。
   The first person was Jessica.　　　　　　　　　　(to finish the work)

2. コンピュータは英語を学ぶための便利な道具です。
   The computer is a useful tool.　　　　　　　　　(to learn English)

3. その学生はアドバイスをくれる人を探しています。
   The student is looking for someone.　　　　　　(to give him advice)

4. 体重を減らす２つの良い方法はダイエットと運動です。
   Two good ways are diet and exercise.　　　　　(to lose weight)

5. 私達は友達がいるのでトルコに行く計画を立てました。
   We made a plan because I have a friend there.　(to go to Turkey)

B 日本語の文に合うように語句を並びかえて英文を完成させ、全文を書きましょう。

1. 高木夫妻は世界一周旅行をするのに十分なお金がある。
   [around / enough / have / money / Mr. and Mrs. Takagi / travel / the world / to].

2. パーティに着て行くものが何もない。
   [for / have / I / nothing / party / to / the / wear].

C 下線部の働きが形容詞的、副詞的のどちらかを考えて○をつけましょう。

1. We were surprised <u>to hear the proposal</u>.　　　形容詞的／副詞的
2. He has five things <u>to do by 3 o'clock</u>.　　　形容詞的／副詞的
3. I can give you something <u>to drink</u> if you are thirsty.　　　形容詞的／副詞的
4. I went to the post office this morning <u>to buy stamps</u>.　　　形容詞的／副詞的
5. They didn't have the energy <u>to walk back home</u>.　　　形容詞的／副詞的

D （　）に適切な語を入れて文を完成させましょう。

1. 私にはその問題について考える時間がなかった。

   I had no (　　　) (　　　) (　　　) about the problem.

2. 私たちはコンサートで歌う歌を10曲選んだ。

   We have chosen ten (　　　) (　　　) (　　　) at the concert.

3. デビッドは来週の月曜日までにしなければならない宿題がたくさんある。

   David has a lot of (　　　) (　　　) (　　　) by next Monday.

4. あなたにお会いする機会があって嬉しいです。

   I'm happy to have a (　　　) (　　　) (　　　) you.

5. 私には助けてくれる友達がたくさんいます。

   I have a lot of (　　　) (　　　) (　　　) me.

E 博物館で見た展示についての文章を読んで、問題に答えましょう。

Last Friday, I went to a museum to see an exhibition called "The World of Kimono in the Edo period." The exhibition was displaying not only kimonos but also a lot of beautiful accessories to use with kimonos. Among them, I particularly liked the *netsuke* and *inro* used by men. *Inro* is a container to put small things like medicine in. As a kimono has no pockets, men used to hang *inro* from the *obi* with a cord. *Netsuke* is a thing to stop *inro* from dropping from the *obi*. It was attached to the end of the cord and was hooked at the top of the *obi*. I loved the beauty of these handicrafts. The exhibition was great and gave me a chance to learn about traditional Japanese arts and crafts.

注) **used to** 〜したものだった　　　**be attached to** 〜に取り付けられている
　　be hooked 引っかけられている　　　**handicraft** 手工芸品

1. 形容詞の働きをする to 不定詞を○で囲み、修飾される名詞に下線を引きましょう。

2. a 〜 d の内、印籠と根付はどれでしょう。
   印籠　_____
   根付　_____

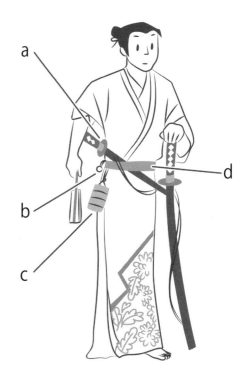

Unit 18 形容詞の働きをする（4）関係代名詞節 - 1

> 関係代名詞は、接続詞と代名詞の働きを持つ語です。関係代名詞を含む節には、その前の名詞（先行詞）を修飾する形容詞の働きがあります。先行詞が人の場合の関係代名詞には who、whose、whom などがあります。

a woman **who** wrote the song　　　その歌を書いた 女性
先行詞
　　　接続詞 + she
　　　　　She wrote the song.

◇（　　）に適切な語句を入れましょう。

主格　　I know a boy **who** has 7 sisters.

　　　　　　　He has 7 sisters.

　　　　私は（　　　　　　　　　　　）を知っています。

所有格　I know a boy **whose** sister lives in London.

　　　　　　　His sister lives in London.

　　　　私は（　　　　　　　　　　　）を知っています。

目的格　I know a boy **whom** you taught last semester.

　　　　　　　You taught **him** last semester.

　　　　私は（　　　　　　　　　　　）を知っています。

A （　　）に入る関係代名詞が主格なら who、所有格なら whose、目的格なら whom を入れましょう。

1. I'm going to call a friend. I haven't seen him for a long time.
   → I'm going to call a friend (　　　　) I haven't seen for a long time.
2. We helped the old woman. Her bag looked very heavy.
   → We helped the old woman (　　　　) bag looked very heavy.
3. The hospital is looking for nurses. They can speak Chinese.
   → The hospital is looking for nurses (　　　　) can speak Chinese.

B （　　）に入る語句をリストの中からすべて選びましょう。

> buy   daughter   drink   my daughter   make
> old dog   the old dog

1. I know some women who (　　　　) vegetable juice every day.
   _____

2. The man whose (　　　　) was sick left his office early yesterday.
   _____

3. The shop owner whom (　　　　) likes is kind to everyone.
   _____

C 日本語の文に合うように語句を並びかえて英文を完成させ、全文を書きましょう。文頭の文字が小文字表記になっている場合があります。

1. 私達は家が燃えてしまった近所の人の為にお金を集めています。
   [are / burned down / collecting / house / money / for the neighbor / we / whose].

2. ブラウンさんは彼が昨日電話をした女性からEメールを受け取りました。
   [an e-mail / called / from / got / he / Mr. Brown / the woman / whom] yesterday.

3. 自転車に乗った警察官が道で私を呼びとめました。
   [a bicycle / a police officer / me / on / riding / stopped / was / who] on the street.

D 英文を日本語に訳しましょう。

1. The author whose books are translated into 40 languages is going to give a lecture at this university.

2. We call a person who starts a business an "entrepreneur."

3. The two employees whom we hired in April have already quit.

4. One of the astronauts who landed on the moon died in 2012.

E 月の名前の語源について述べた文章を読んで、問題に答えましょう。

　　How many months do we have in a year? That is an easy question. Twelve, of course. But do you know the origins of their names? Well, some of the months were named after gods or goddesses. Mars, the Roman god of war, is one god whose name was given to a month. He gave his name to the third month of the year. How about people? Are there any people whose names became the names of months? Yes, there are two. Who are they? One is the man who became the first emperor of the Roman Empire – Augustus Caesar. As you can probably guess, August was named after him. The other person whose name is still found in the name of a month is Julius Caesar. He gave his name to the month before August.

注) **origin** 起源　　　**emperor** 皇帝

1. 関係代名詞節を○で囲み、修飾される名詞（先行詞）に下線を引きましょう。

2. 次の質問に英語で答えましょう。

　a. What is the name of the month named after the Roman god of war?

　　_____

　b. Who was the first emperor of the Roman Empire?

　　_____

　c. What month is named after Julius Caesar?

　　_____

Unit 19 形容詞の働きをする (5) 関係代名詞節 - 2

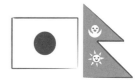

先行詞が人間以外の場合の関係代名詞には which、whose などがあります。

◇（　　　）に適切な語句を入れましょう。

主格　　　I have a <u>book</u> |which has 500 pages|.

　　　　　　　　　　　　　　It has 500 pages.

　　　　　私は（　　　　　　　　　　　）本を持っています。

所有格　　I have a <u>book</u> |whose cover is red|.

　　　　　　　　　　　　　　Its cover is red.

　　　　　私は（　　　　　　　　　　　）本を持っています。

目的格　　I have a <u>book</u> |which Tom wrote|.

　　　　　　　　　　　　　　Tom wrote it.

　　　　　私は（　　　　　　　　　　　）本を持っています。

* 関係代名詞 that は、who（主格）、whom（目的格）、which（主格／目的格）の代わりに使うことができます。
  I know a <u>boy</u> **who** has 7 sisters. = I know a <u>boy</u> **that** has 7 sisters.
  I have a <u>book</u> **which** Tom wrote. = I have a <u>book</u> **that** Tom wrote.

* 目的格の関係代名詞 whom、which、that は省略することもできます。
  I know a <u>boy</u> **whom/that** you taught last year.=I know a <u>boy</u> **you** taught last year.
  I have a <u>book</u> **which/that** Tom wrote. =I have a <u>book</u> Tom wrote.

* 関係代名詞 what は先行詞なしで使います。
  ◇（　　　）に適切な語句を入れましょう。
  This is **what** I wanted.　　これは（　　　　　　　　　）です。
  =This is **the thing which** I wanted.

A 上の2文と下の文が同じ内容になるように、(　　) に which または whose を入れましょう。

1. I'm looking for a house. Its front door is green.
   → I'm looking for a house (　　　) front door is green.

2. The movie was boring. I watched it with my family
   → The movie (　　　) I watched with my family was boring.

3. We bought a dog. It has black spots on its back.
   → We bought a dog (　　　) has black spots on its back.

B (　　) に which, whose または what を入れて文を完成させて、日本語に訳しましょう。

1. The fish (　　　) my husband caught at the lake tasted great.
   _____

2. My son needs an alarm clock (　　　) makes a loud noise.
   _____

3. I like (　　　) I ate for breakfast today.
   _____

4. Nepal is the only country (　　　) national flag is not rectangular or square.
   _____

5. (　　　) I'm going to tell you is a secret.
   _____

C

( ) に入れることができるものを、リストから [ ] 内の数だけ選びましょう。Ø は関係代名詞の省略を示します。

> who   whose   whom   which   that   what   Ø

1. The teacher gave the advice (/   ) changed my life. [2]
2. The kitten (/   /   ) my mother found in front of our house was black. [3]
3. My brother regrets (   ) he has done to his girlfriend. [1]
4. The man (/   ) made a lot of money in business got married to a beautiful woman. [2]
5. My sister works for a company (   ) employees must speak English. [1]

D

( ) に入れるのに最も適切なものをリストから選び文を完成させましょう。同じ語句を繰り返し使う事はできません。

> whose father is very rich
> what I borrowed from you
> who has to leave his team
> which you showed to us while we were in Sapporo

1. We are sorry for the soccer player _____ because of his injury.
2. Thank you for the kindness _____.
3. I haven't returned _____.
4. The girl _____ spends ¥100,000 on her clothes every month.

E ある街で開かれたマラソンについての文章を読んで、問題に答えましょう。 CD 20

　Last Sunday there was a big marathon which 20,000 people attended. Runners enjoyed the course which included the castle, the river, the main street and many popular places. They started from the old castle which is in the center of the city. The trees that are planted by the river gave runners some pleasant shade. The runners felt very excited to run in the middle of the main street which usually only cars occupy. Volunteers served a lot of things that the runners could eat and drink along the course. They also cheered them on with placards that said, "Hang in there!" "Do your best!" or "We are with you!" The marathon ended with the last runner that crossed the finish line at 6:30:15. It was a great day not only for runners but also for spectators.

注) occupy　占領する　　　　　spectator　観客

1. 関係代名詞に下線を引き、省略できるものを○で囲みましょう。
2. 本文に合うように、(　　　)に適切な語を入れましょう。ただし、余分な語句が含まれています。

> castle　　last　　main street　　river　　shade
> spectators　　volunteers

　a. A runner finished the course at 6:30:15. He came in (　　　　　).
　b. In the morning, runners got together at the (　　　　　) and the race started.
　c. The (　　　　　) of the trees by the river was a relief for runners.
　d. Snacks and drinks that (　　　　　) offered gave the runners a lot of energy.
　e. Some runners ran in the center of the (　　　　　) for the first time. Usually people can't run there because it is full of cars.

Unit 20 名詞の働きをする（1） to 不定詞

> to 不定詞は、名詞の働きをして、主語・目的語・補語になることがあります。

◇（　）に適切な日本語を入れましょう。

主語　**To study** every day is important.　（　　　　　　　　）は重要です。

目的語　I like **to swim**.　私は（　　　　　　　　）が好きです。

補語　My job is **to teach** math.　私の仕事は（　　　　　　　　）です。

＊to 不定詞を用いた構文には次のようなものがあります。

◇英文を日本語に訳しましょう。
- It … to ～　「～することは…だ」
  It was easy **to find** the restaurant.

  _____

- want / tell / ask A to ～　「A に～してもらいたい／するように言う／するように頼む」
  I **asked** him **to come** here at one o'clock.

  _____

「to 不定詞」のまとめ

◇（　）に適切な日本語を入れましょう。

副詞の働き　I went to America **to study** English.
　　　　　私は（　　　　　　　　）アメリカに行きました。

形容詞の働き　I found a person **to teach** us yoga.
　　　　　私は（　　　　　　　　）を見つけました。

名詞の働き　I started **to read** the book.
　　　　　私は（　　　　　　　　）始めました。

下線部の to 不定詞が形容詞的用法、副詞的用法、名詞的用法のどれかを考えて○をつけましょう。

1. <u>To take</u> a walk in the morning makes me happy.

   　　　　　　　　　　　　　　　　　　　　　形容詞的／副詞的／名詞的

2. Autumn is the best season <u>to visit</u> Kyoto.　　形容詞的／副詞的／名詞的

3. I am going to climb the mountain <u>to enjoy</u> fresh air.

   　　　　　　　　　　　　　　　　　　　　　形容詞的／副詞的／名詞的

4. Kana often forgets <u>to bring</u> her textbook to class.

   　　　　　　　　　　　　　　　　　　　　　形容詞的／副詞的／名詞的

 英文中の to が必要な場所に∧を入れて日本語に訳しましょう。

1. Master a foreign language takes a lot of time.

   _____

2. My dream is be a professional baseball player.

   _____

3. The girl living far from the university decided move into the dormitory.

   _____

4. My sister is trying sell the ring she got for her birthday.

   _____

5. It is illegal park a car on this street.

   _____

6. Paul asked me repair his broken motorbike.

   _____

C

日本語の文に合うように語句を並びかえて英文を完成させ、全文を書きましょう。文頭の文字が小文字表記になっている場合があります。

1. 私は10才の時から外国で勉強したいと思っていました。
   [abroad / have / I / since / study / to / wanted] I was ten.

___

2. 私の仕事はお客様からの電話に答える事です。
   [answer / customers / from / is / job / my / the phone calls / to].

___

3. 私の父は、運転する時は気を付けるようにいつも私に言います。
   [always / be / father / me / my / careful / tells / to] when I drive.

___

4. 昼食後に昼寝をすることは気分をさわやかにしてくれる。
   It [after / a nap / is / lunch / refreshing / take / to].

___

D 英文を日本語に訳しましょう。

1. The student decided to work on weekends to buy a computer.

___

2. I don't want my mother to throw away the comic books I bought when I was in junior high school.

___

3. It is more expensive to repair the bike than to buy a new one.

___

E クラブの合宿のお知らせを読んで、問題に答えましょう。 21

TAIKO DRUMS SUMMER CAMP (AUGUST 5 – AUGUST 8)

The purpose of this *Taiko* Drums Summer Camp is to help club members to improve their *taiko* skills. In the morning, members will practice in small groups to develop basic skills. In the afternoon, all the members will get together and practice selected *taiko* music. Also, every morning before the morning session, members will work out to get stronger as the whole body is used in *taiko*. Members will have three delicious meals per day. Two members will share a room. Members will be required to take a *taiko* skills test at the end of the camp and to write a three-page paper about what they have learned.

注) **improve** 〜を向上させる　　　**work out** 運動する
　　be required to 〜することを要求される

1. 名詞の働きをする to 不定詞の句を○で囲みましょう。

2. 上の英文を参考にして、日本語の「お知らせ」を完成させましょう。

```
和太鼓　夏合宿

目的　　　_____こと
日程　　　_____
練習内容　午前：_____
　　　　　_____
　　　　　午後：_____
宿泊　　　___人１部屋。食事は_____

参加者は以下のことが求められます。
　・_____こと
　・_____こと
```

Unit 21 名詞の働きをする（2）動名詞

> 動名詞は動詞の原形＋~ing で作ります。現在分詞と同じ形ですが、働きは違います。動名詞は名詞の働きをして、主語、補語、目的語になります。

◇（　　　）に適切な日本語を入れましょう。

主語　　　Swimming in the river is a lot of fun.
　　　　　（　　　　　　　　　　　　　　　　）はとても楽しいです。

目的語　　The girl stopped eating cake.
　　　　　その少女は（　　　　　　　　　　）をやめました。

補語　　　My job is teaching history.
　　　　　私の仕事は（　　　　　　　　　　）です。

＊動詞には目的語に動名詞をとるもの、不定詞をとるもの、両方とるものがあります。

A. 動名詞のみをとる動詞	enjoy　finish　avoid　stop　　　など
B. 不定詞のみをとる動詞	decide　need　plan　want　　　など
C. どちらもとる動詞	begin　continue　like　start　　など

例）〇 I enjoyed singing.　　　✕ I enjoyed to sing.

＊前置詞の後に動詞を持ってくる時は動名詞になります。

◇（　　　）に適切な日本語を入れましょう。

I am interested in reading English books.
私は（　　　　　　　　　　　　　　）興味があります。

I am thinking about borrowing money from my father.
私は（　　　　　　　　　　　　　　）考えています。

下線部が動名詞、現在分詞のどちらかを考えて○をつけましょう。

1. Luke's sister is <u>helping</u> poor people in Africa.　　　動名詞／現在分詞
2. Luke's dream is <u>helping</u> poor people in Africa.　　　動名詞／現在分詞
3. Luke is very good at <u>making</u> a speech.　　　動名詞／現在分詞
4. Luke is the man <u>making</u> a speech on the stage now.　動名詞／現在分詞
5. Luke started <u>making</u> a speech after he was introduced.

　　　　　　　　　　　　　　　　　　　　　　　　　　　動名詞／現在分詞

 （　　）内から適切な語句をすべて選び、○をつけましょう。

1. Thank you for (send, to send, sent, sending) me a birthday card.
2. Many young people like (go, to go, went, going) to clubs to dance.
3. Jill can (swim, to swim, swimming, swims) 1 km in 15 minutes.
4. I have already finished (clean, to clean, cleaning, cleaned) my room.
5. George wanted (finish, to finish, finished, finishing) his homework by 5.
6. (Work, To work, Worked, Working) late is tiring.

 日本語の文に合うように語句を並びかえて英文を完成させ、全文を書きましょう。文頭の文字が小文字表記になっている場合があります。

1. 毎朝新鮮なフルーツジュースを飲むことはあなたの健康によい。
   [for / good / drinking / every morning / health / is / fresh fruit juice / your].

   _____

2. ミドリは英語の本を辞書を使わずに読もうとした。
   [an English book / a dictionary / Midori / read / to / tried / using / without].

   _____

D 各文の続きとして最も適切なものをリストから選び文を完成させ、日本語に訳しましょう。同じ語句を繰り返し使う事はできません。

---
playing baseball now belongs to the music club
hearing from you
reading novels and painting pictures
traveling abroad was very expensive
---

1. Our teacher's hobbies are _____.

2. When our grandparents were young, _____.

3. I'm looking forward to _____.

4. The student who stopped _____.

E 動名詞を使って、自由に英文を完成させましょう。

1. My hobby is _____.

2. I hate _____.

F ある学生が書いたメールとそれに対する返事を読んで、問題に答えましょう。 22

Dear Sir/Madam,

　I'm a university student majoring in French. I am enjoying learning French very much and I'm interested in taking a conversation class in the evening on Thursday or Saturday. I just started learning the language a few months ago, so I'm still a beginner. Do you have any classes for me? Please send me the schedule for the next term.
Many thanks,
Alicia Williams

Dear Ms. Williams,

　Thank you for your inquiry. Our schedule for the next term is:

	Tuesday	Wednesday	Thursday	Friday	Saturday
6:40 - 7:40	Conversation Intermediate	Conversation Beginner	Reading Intermediate	Reading Advanced	Grammar Beginner
7:50 - 8:50	Grammar Intermediate	Conversation Advanced	Conversation Beginner	Reading Beginner	Conversation Intermediate

　The new term starts in a month. You can take a free trial lesson before making any decisions. If you have any questions, please do not hesitate to contact me. I am looking forward to hearing from you soon.
Best wishes,
Dan Suzuki
OPD Language Academy

注）inquiry　問い合わせ　　　　　hesitate to　～するのをためらう

1. 動名詞を○で囲みましょう。

2. 本文に合うように、（　　）に適切な語を入れましょう。
　アリシアは⁽ᵃ⁾（　　　　　）のクラスのことを聞くため⁽ᵇ⁾（　　　　　）宛てにメールを書いた。彼女はクラスを取るとしたら⁽ᶜ⁾（　　　）曜日の⁽ᵈ⁾（　　　）からのクラスをとるだろう。新学期は⁽ᵉ⁾（　　　　　）に始まる。

Unit 22 名詞の働きをする（3）that 節と疑問詞節

> that（接続詞）＋節は名詞の働きをして、主語・目的語・補語になる事があります。

◇（　　）に適切な日本語を入れましょう。

主語　That you will pass the test is certain.
　　　（　　　　　　　　　　　　　　　　）は確かだ。

目的語　I know that you passed the test .
　　　　私は（　　　　　　　　　　　　）知っている。

補語　The problem is that you cheated .
　　　問題は（　　　　　　　　　　　　　　　）だ。

＊ that 節を目的語にとる動詞には、think, know, hear, hope, expect, believe などがあります。that 節が目的語や補語になる場合、that を省略することが出来ます。

> 疑問詞も接続詞の働きをして、疑問詞節が名詞の働きをする事があります。疑問詞は節の一番前にきます。

例）**where** you met him, **when** she came, **what** he bought

I don't know **where you met him**. 私はあなたが彼にどこで会ったか知りません。

◇（　　）に適切な日本語を入れましょう。

主語　Who stole my bag is clear. （　　　　　　　　　）は明らかだ。

目的語　I know why she didn't come . 私は（　　　　　　　）知っている。

補語　The question is what time he will be back .
　　　　　　　　　　　　　問題は（　　　　　　　　　　　　）だ。

＊ that / 疑問詞＋節を用いた構文には次のようなものがあります。
　　・It … that / 疑問詞 ～　　　　～は…だ。
　　　It is certain **that** you will pass the test.
　　　It is clear **who** stole my bag.

A 日本語の文に合うように、(　　) に that か疑問詞を入れましょう。

1. 明日は大雨だと思います。

   I think (　　) it will rain heavily tomorrow.

2. 彼はどこでそのシャツを買ったんだろう。

   I wonder (　　) he bought the shirt.

3. どうやってそこに着くかは重要ではない。

   (　　) we get there is not important.

4. 私の兄は私に母にもっと電話するべきだと言った。

   My brother told me (　　) I should call our mother more often.

5. 明日の午後、台風が九州を直撃するようだ。

   It is likely (　　) the typhoon will hit Kyushu tomorrow afternoon.

B (　　) 内の語句が入る場所に∧を入れて、全文を日本語に訳しましょう。

1. It is great you have saved enough money to travel around the world.　　　(that)

   _____

2. The tourists asked me they should take to Meiji Shrine.　(which bus)

   _____

3. No one knows broke the bench in the park.　　　(who)

   _____

4. He disappeared is a mystery.　　　(why)

   _____

5. The truth is I didn't want my friends to call me Cutie.　　　(that)

   _____

C 文の間違いを正して全文を書き直しましょう。

1. Where is he from is not so important.

2. I don't know what sport does he like.

3. I promise that will never tell a lie.

D 日本語の文に合うように語句を並びかえて英文を完成させましょう。文頭の文字が小文字表記になっている場合があります。

1. 私達はあなたがスイスで楽しい時を過ごすことを願っています。
   [a great time / have / hope / in Switzerland / that / we / will / you].

2. いつどこで彼が生まれたかは明らかではない。
   [and / born / he / isn't / was / when / where] clear.

3. 出口はどこか知りたい。
   [I / is / know / the exit / to / want / where].

4. 我々が環境を破壊しているのは確かだ。
   It [are / certain / destroying / is / that / the environment / we].

5. 私たちは誰がリーダーになるべきか話し合った。
   [about / be / should / talked / the leader / we / who].

E クイズを読んで、問題に答えましょう。 🎧 23

It's the only rock that we eat every day. It's something that animals need to eat, too. Did you know that many of the roads in America were once paths that animals made to get to this rock? Scientists now know why we need to eat this rock. It is very important for our body's functioning. This rock was very valuable, so soldiers were paid their salary with it. In fact, the word "salary" came from the Latin word for this rock. You may think that it is gold or silver, but it's not. Here's a final hint. It makes potato chips, popcorn and miso soup very delicious. Can you guess what this rock is?

注) **functioning** 機能

1. 名詞節を作る that と疑問詞を○で囲みましょう。

2. このクイズの答えを日本語で書きましょう。
   _____

3. 2の答えについて述べているものには T、そうでないものには F を（　　）に書きましょう。
   a. (　　) It can be found in seawater.
   b. (　　) When we sweat, we lose some of it.
   c. (　　) We use it to make strawberry jam.
   d. (　　) It is said that we should take about 50g of it a day.
   e. (　　) Sumo wrestlers throw it before a match.

暗唱文 (recitation)

Unit 2
1. Time flies. — 光陰矢のごとし（時は飛んでいく）。
2. The question is difficult. — その質問は難しい。
3. I won the first prize. — 私は一等賞を勝ち取った。
4. My parents teach me English. — 私の両親は私に英語を教えてくれる。
5. I call my sister Dee. — 私は私の妹をディーと呼んでいる。
6. Akira can swim fast. — アキラは速く泳ぐことができる。
7. My uncle is a doctor. — 私の叔父は医者だ。
8. She speaks Spanish. — 彼女はスペイン語を話す。
9. I bought him a ticket. — 私は彼にチケットを買った。
10. The movie makes me sad. — その映画は私を悲しくさせる。

Unit 3
1. We like our school. — 私達は自分達の学校が好きだ。
2. His father asked her a question. — 彼の父は彼女に質問をした。
3. You made him angry. — あなたは彼を怒らせた。
4. Their teacher told them a story. — 彼らの先生は彼らに物語を語った。
5. Her cats look sleepy. — 彼女の猫達は眠そうだ。
6. Kyoto is famous for its temples. — 京都は寺院で有名だ。
7. You and I are good friends. — あなたと私はよい友達だ。
8. My father often takes a walk with me. — 私の父はよく私と散歩をする。
9. The company sent e-mail to its customers. — その会社は顧客にEメールを送った。
10. He took care of us. — 彼は私達の世話をした。

Unit 4
1. My son usually gets up at 7. — 私の息子はたいてい7時に起きる。
2. Tom and I are brothers. — トムと私は兄弟だ。
3. I studied for 2 hours last night. — 私は昨夜2時間勉強した。
4. Mark read a magazine at the library. — マークは図書館で雑誌を読んだ。
5. The doctors were very busy this morning. — 医者達は今朝とても忙しかった。
6. I'll call you later. — 後であなたに電話します。
7. We are going to eat out tonight. — 私達は今晩外食します。
8. The students come to school early. — その学生達は早く学校に来る。
9. I saw beautiful flowers in the garden. — 私は庭で美しい花々を見た。
10. It will rain tonight. — 今晩雨が降るだろう。

Unit 5

1. My father can cook well. 私の父は料理がうまい。
2. You can eat the cake. そのケーキを食べてもいいよ。
3. Ted may be absent today. テッドは今日欠席かもしれない。
4. You must follow the rules. あなたはルールを守らなければいけない。
5. The bag must be heavy. そのかばんは重いに違いない。
6. Jimmy is able to skateboard well. ジミーはスケートボードが上手い。
7. The students have to clean their rooms. 学生達は自分達の部屋を掃除しなければいけない。
8. We should wash the dishes now. 私達は皿を今洗うべきだ。
9. The girl has to take a make-up test. その少女は追試を受けなければならない。
10. I am able to drive a bus. 私はバスを運転できる。

Unit 6

1. John is making a presentation now. ジョンは今プレゼンをしている。
2. My parents are travel(l)ing in Hokkaido. 私の両親は北海道を旅行中だ。
3. I was talking to my teacher at that time. 私はその時先生と話していた。
4. The stars were shining brightly. 星が明るく輝いていた。
5. He will still be sleeping at 11a.m. 彼は朝11時はまだ寝ているだろう。
6. I'm looking for my wallet. 私は自分の財布を探している。
7. She will be working at the convenience store tomorrow. 彼女は明日は、コンビニで働いているだろう。
8. The boy was having a good time at the party. その少年はパーティで楽しんでいた。
9. Beth and Jo were shopping together. ベスとジョーは一緒に買い物をしていた。
10. They will be playing baseball tomorrow afternoon. 彼らは明日の午後、野球をしているだろう。

Unit 7

1. The church was built in 1932. その教会は1932年に建てられた。
2. The room is cleaned once a week. その部屋は週に1回清掃されます。
3. Newspapers are delivered at 4 a.m. 新聞は午前4時に配達される。
4. The meeting is going to be held next Friday. その会議は次の金曜日に開かれる。
5. The coach is trusted by the players. そのコーチは選手に信頼されている。
6. The dresses were designed by my cousin. そのドレスは私のいとこによってデザインされた。
7. Three students are given the award every year. 3人の学生が毎年その賞を与えられる。
8. The twins were named Sara and Anna by their parents. その双子は両親によってサラとアンナと名付けられた。

9. The book will be found in this section. その本はこのセクションにあるでしょう。
10. The soccer player is known all around the world. そのサッカー選手は世界中で知られている。

Unit 8

1. I have never heard of it. そのことを聞いたことがない。
2. Jessica has been in Tokyo since last Tuesday. ジェシカはこの前の火曜日以来東京にいる。
3. I have seen the movie three times. 私はその映画を3回見た。
4. The guests have just arrived. 客がちょうど到着したところだ。
5. I have lost my wallet. 私は財布をなくしてしまった。
6. Susan has already found an apartment. スーザンはすでにアパートを見つけている。
7. We have been to Cambodia twice. 私達は2回カンボジアに行ったことがある。
8. My French friend has gone back to Paris. 私のフランス人の友人はパリに帰ってしまった。
9. It has been cold since last week. 先週以来寒い。
10. Ryo has wanted a kitten for a long time. 遼は長い間子猫を欲しがっている。

Unit 9

1. Kathy isn't eating lunch now. キャシーは今昼食中ではない。
2. I don't drink coffee. 私はコーヒーは飲まない。
3. The club doesn't have enough members. そのクラブには十分な部員がいない。
4. I didn't watch the program last night. 私は昨夜その番組を見なかった。
5. The leaves haven't turned red yet. 木の葉はまだ赤くなっていない。
6. I can't remember the password. パスワードを思い出せない。
7. It will not rain tomorrow. 明日は、雨は降らないだろう。
8. These shoes were not so expensive. これらの靴はそれほど高くなかった。
9. I haven't checked the weather forecast. 天気予報をチェックしていない。
10. You don't have to wait for me. 私を待たなくてもいいよ。

Unit 10

1. Did you change your hairstyle? 髪型を変えた？
2. Has the 12:30 train left? 12時30分の電車は出ましたか？
3. Where do you buy vegetables? 野菜はどこで買いますか？
4. How tall are you? あなたの身長は？

5. When were the first Olympic Games held? 最初のオリンピックはいつ開かれましたか？
6. Does he have to stay home tonight? 彼は今夜、家にいなければなりませんか？
7. Are the tickets still available? チケットはまだ入手可能ですか？
8. What color is your bicycle? あなたの自転車は何色ですか？
9. How can I improve my English? 私はどうすれば英語を上達させられますか？
10. May I leave my suitcase here? ここに私のスーツケースを置いておいてもいいですか？

Unit 11   33

1. My puppy is as small as this ball. 私の子犬はこのボールぐらい小さい。
2. Mars isn't as big as Earth. 火星は地球ほど大きくない。
3. I finished my work as soon as possible. 私はできるだけ早く仕事を終えた。
4. August is hotter than September. 8月は9月より暑い。
5. Buses are more useful than trains in this city. この市ではバスは電車より便利だ。
6. Ann came to the office (the) earliest. アンは一番早く事務所に来た。
7. I can work better in the morning than in the afternoon. 私は午後より午前のほうが仕事がよくできる。
8. He has published more books than the author. 彼はその作家より多くの本を出版している。
9. This is the most expensive watch in my store. これは私の店で一番高い時計だ。
10. I bought the cheapest umbrella of the five. 私は5つの中で一番安い傘を買った。

Unit 12   34

1. I'll see you on Thursday. 木曜日に会いましょう。
2. We walked along the path. 私達は小道に沿って歩いた。
3. I have studied French for two years. 私はフランス語を勉強して2年になる。
4. I wrote my name with a pen. 私はペンで自分の名前を書いた。
5. We had to be at the airport by 7:30. 私達は空港に7時30分までに行かなければならなかった。
6. Ken and I usually speak in English. 健と私はたいてい英語で話す。
7. She was sitting behind him. 彼女は彼の後ろに座っていました。
8. I'll be waiting for you at that corner. あの角であなたを待っています。
9. We walked from the station to the mall. 私達は駅からモールまで歩いた。
10. I put the shopping list on the refrigerator. 私はその買い物リストを冷蔵庫の上にはった。

Unit 13

1. I was shocked to hear the news. 　私はそのニュースを聞いてショックを受けた。
2. We went to Chicago to see our daughter. 　私達は娘に会いにシカゴに行った。
3. Julia boiled water to make tea. 　ジュリアはお茶を入れるため水を沸かした。
4. John is glad to be back home. 　ジョンは家に戻れて喜んでいる。
5. The coffee was too hot to drink. 　そのコーヒーは熱過ぎて飲めなかった。
6. The boy was kind enough to show me the way. 　その少年は親切にも私達に道を教えてくれた。
7. The bag is small enough to fit under the seat. 　そのかばんは席の下に収まるのに十分小さい。
8. Daniel is going to call his grandmother to say happy birthday. 　ダニエルはお誕生日おめでとうと言うために祖母に電話するつもりです。
9. Bill will be surprised to see a lot of people there. 　ビルはそこでたくさんの人を見てびっくりするでしょう。
10. The problem may be too difficult to solve in an hour. 　その問題は難しすぎて1時間では解けないかもしれない。

Unit 14

1. My sister gets up after I leave for work. 　妹は私が仕事に出掛けた後に起きる。
2. I leave for work before my sister gets up. 　私は妹が起きる前に仕事に出掛ける。
3. You should lock the door when you go out. 　あなたは出掛ける時ドアに鍵を掛けるべきだ。
4. Beth turned on the heater because she felt cold. 　ベスは寒かったのでヒーターをつけた。
5. If you have any questions, please contact us at 555-0101. 　もし質問があれば、555-0101に連絡下さい。
6. Although the hotel is very old, the rooms are clean. 　そのホテルはとても古いけれども部屋はきれいだ。
7. Someone called you while you were taking a bath. 　あなたがお風呂に入っている間に誰かが電話してきましたよ。
8. We will wait here until you arrive. 　あなたが到着するまで私達はここで待ちます。
9. When I was a child, I didn't like spiders. 　子供の頃私は蜘蛛が好きでなかった。
10. I've always wanted a pet since I was a child. 　私は子供の頃からずっとペットを欲しいと思っています。

Unit 15 　CD 37

1. My birthday is the day after tomorrow. 　私の誕生日は明後日です。
2. Nancy walks to the library in her neighborhood. 　ナンシーは近所の図書館に歩いていく。
3. A toy like this is popular. 　このようなおもちゃが人気です。
4. The train for Tokyo has already left. 　東京行きの列車はもう出発しました。
5. You can eat the cookies in the box. 　箱の中のクッキーを食べてもいいよ。
6. I live in a house with a big garden. 　私は大きな庭付きの家に住んでいる。
7. A stranger showed me the way to the station. 　見知らぬ人が駅への道を教えてくれた。
8. I read an interesting story about global warming. 　僕は地球温暖化についてのおもしろい話を読んだ。
9. The restaurants on the 7th floor are open until 11 p.m. 　7階にあるレストランは夜11時まで開いています。
10. Beijing is the capital city of China. 　北京は中国の首都です。

Unit 16 　CD 38

1. The man wearing a red tie is my father. 　赤いネクタイをしている男性は私の父です。
2. I watched a video clip of a dancing baby. 　私は踊っている赤ちゃんのビデオを見ました。
3. The teacher patted the sleeping student. 　先生は寝ている学生を軽くたたいた。
4. I'm looking forward to the reunion held next March. 　私は来年の3月に開かれる同窓会を楽しみにしています。
5. Boiled eggs are easy to make. 　ゆで卵は作るのが簡単だ。
6. Bob is still using the broken umbrella. 　ボブはまだ壊れた傘を使っている。
7. The picture hanging on the wall was painted by my mother. 　壁に掛かっている絵は私の母によって描かれたものだ。
8. Yuri talked to the man sitting next to her. 　ゆりは隣に座っている男性に話しかけた。
9. My cousin collects comic books published in the 1970s. 　私のいとこは1970年代に出版されたマンガを集めている。
10. The kitten found in front of my house looks very weak. 　私の家の前で見つかった子猫はとても弱っているように見える。

Unit 17 　CD 39

1. The last person to leave the room should turn off the lights. 　部屋を出る最後の人が電気を消すべきだ。
2. Paul has the ability to solve the problem. 　ポールにはその問題を解決する能力がある。
3. The teacher gave us a lot of homework 　先生は来週までにしなければいけない宿

to do by next week.
4. We need five people to help us.
5. What is the best way to learn English?
6. Ms. Brown is looking for a person to clean her garden.
7. I have something to tell you.
8. I didn't have time to rewrite the paper.
9. Mr. and Mrs. Tanaka made a decision to sell their house.
10. They have already found a band to play at the festival.

題をたくさん私達に与えた。
私達は手伝ってくれる人が5人必要だ。
英語を学ぶ一番いい方法は何ですか。
ブラウンさんは彼女の庭をきれいにしてくれる人を探している。
あなたに言いたい事があります。
私は小論文を書き直す時間がなかった。
田中夫妻は家を売る決心をした。

彼らはもうすでに祭りで演奏してくれるバンドを見つけた。

Unit 18   CD 40

1. Mr. Doi is taking care of a boy whose parents are in America.
2. Mike met a man who runs three restaurants in New York.
3. This dictionary is for people who are learning English.
4. I like people who are energetic and independent.
5. The artist whose works are in the museum is going to give a lecture tomorrow.
6. Many foreigners who like manga visit Japan.
7. The student whose house is far from school is often late.
8. I have a friend whose father runs a bakery.
9. Tim hired a person whom I recommended.
10. The children whom Mr. Tanaka is teaching are very smart.

土井さんは両親がアメリカにいる少年の面倒を見ている。
マイクはニューヨークでレストランを3軒経営している人に会った。
この辞書は英語を学んでいる人の為の物です。
私はエネルギッシュで独立心のある人が好きです。
作品がその美術館にある芸術家は明日講義を行います。
マンガ好きの多くの外国人が日本を訪れる。
家が学校から遠いその学生はよく遅刻する。
私には父親がパン屋を営んでいる友達がいます。
ティムは私が推薦した人を雇った。
田中さんが教えている子供達はとても賢い。

Unit 19   CD 41

1. The bread which was baked this morning smells good.
2. I work at the shopping mall which opened last month.

今朝焼かれたパンはいい匂いだ。

私は先月オープンしたショッピングモールで働いている。

3. The house whose roof is broken is 100 years old.　　屋根が壊れているその家は築100年だ。
4. My grandmother is using a cell phone whose buttons are big.　　私の祖母はボタンが大きい携帯電話を使っている。
5. I haven't read the book which my teacher gave me.　　私は先生がくれた本を読んでいない。
6. The only thing that I remember is the man's name.　　私が覚えているのはその人の名前だけだ。
7. I'm going to see the movie that was released two days ago.　　私は2日前に封切りになった映画を見に行く予定だ。
8. We have to be careful with the information we get from the Internet.　　インターネットから得られる情報に私達は注意しなければいけない。
9. The dream I had last night was very strange.　　昨晩見た夢はとても奇妙だった。
10. I'll show you what I like.　　私が好きなものをあなたにお見せしましょう。

Unit 20　　CD 42

1. Martha's dream is to be a lawyer.　　マーサの夢は弁護士になる事だ。
2. The students started to clean their room.　　学生達は自分達の部屋を掃除し始めた。
3. Ms. Russ wants to practice the piano every day.　　ラスさんは毎日ピアノの練習をしたがっている。
4. My goal is to go to the Olympics.　　僕の目標はオリンピックに出る事だ。
5. What you should do first is to get information.　　君が最初にするべき事は情報を得ることだ。
6. It is nice to see you here.　　ここであなたに会えてうれしい。
7. It is dangerous to ride a motorbike in the snow.　　雪の中でバイクに乗るのは危険だ。
8. The teacher told his students to be careful.　　先生は学生達に注意するように言った。
9. Ms. Russ wants us to practice the piano every day.　　ラスさんは私達に毎日ピアノの練習をしてもらいたがっている。
10. I asked Keith to give me a ride to the station.　　私はキースに駅まで車に乗せて行ってくれるように頼んだ。

Unit 21　　CD 43

1. I stopped smoking because it isn't good for my health.　　僕は健康に良くないので煙草を止めた。
2. Getting enough sleep is very important.　　十分な睡眠をとる事はとても大事だ。
3. Travelling in foreign countries is a lot of fun.　　外国旅行はとても楽しい。
4. He avoided meeting the girl on the way to　　彼は学校に行く途中その女の子に会うの

school. | を避けた。
5. Jun enjoys drawing pictures. | 潤は絵を描くのを楽しんでいる。
6. My plan for the summer vacation is going to Paris. | 私の夏休みの計画はパリに行くことだ。
7. Their problem is having too much free time. | 彼らの問題はひまな時間がありすぎる事だ。
8. I'm looking forward to seeing you soon. | あなたにまもなく会える事を楽しみにしています。
9. She achieved her goal by working hard. | 彼女は一生懸命働く事によって目標を達成した。
10. I locked the door before leaving the house. | 僕は家を出る前にドアに鍵をかけた。

Unit 22

1. We say that silence is golden. | 私達は「沈黙は金」と言います。
2. I want to know how she solved the problem. | 私は彼女がどうやってその問題を解いたのか知りたい。
3. I wonder why the students are so excited. | 学生たちはなぜそんなに興奮しているのかなあ。
4. Ted believes that working hard is important. | テッドは一生懸命働くことは大切だと思っている。
5. Sam can't remember where he left his umbrella. | サムは彼がどこに傘を置き忘れたか思い出せない。
6. It is likely that Mr. Tang will get the job. | タン氏がその仕事を得そうだ。
7. They are interested in which team will win the game. | 彼らはどのチームが勝つか興味を持っている。
8. How you look is not everything. | あなたの見かけがすべてではない。
9. The problem is he forgot to call her. | 問題は彼が彼女に電話をするのを忘れたことだ。
10. It is uncertain when we will get the results. | 私達がいつ結果を得るかは確かではない。

TEXT PRODUCTION STAFF

edited by	編集
Eiichi Kanno	菅野 英一
Taiichi Sano	佐野 泰一

English-language editing by	英文校閲
Bill Benfield	ビル・ベンフィールド

illustrated by	イラスト
IOK Co., Ltd.	株式会社 イオック

cover design by	表紙デザイン
Lighthouse Co., Ltd.	株式会社 ライトハウス

CD PRODUCTION STAFF

recorded by	吹き込み者
Bianca Allen (AmE)	ビィアンカ・アレン（アメリカ英語）
Howard Colefield (AmE)	ハワード・コーフィールド（アメリカ英語）

Grammar Made Easy
知っておきたい基礎英文法

2015年1月20日 初版発行
2023年3月30日 第6刷発行

著 者　平田 三樹子・原田 曜子
　　　　Eric Bray

発行者　佐野 英一郎

発行所　株式会社 成美堂
　　　　〒101-0052　東京都千代田区神田小川町3-22
　　　　TEL 03-3291-2261　FAX 03-3293-5490
　　　　https://www.seibido.co.jp

印刷・製本　倉敷印刷（株）

ISBN 978-4-7919-3384-6　　　　Printed in Japan

・落丁・乱丁本はお取り替えします。
・本書の無断複写は、著作権上の例外を除き著作権侵害となります。